The FINAL Chapter Of ABUSE

By: Michelle Taylor

The FINAL Chapter Of ABUSE

My Dedication

To my very best friend that I miss so much: Tammy Ann. I just want you to know that I love you with all my heart. I also want you to know that you were right about everything you said to me once, that when I finished making that home he and I had into a doll house then he would be done with me. I also want you to know that you were right about him never loving me. Edward was never a husband like your husband Brent. I will never forget all the trips that we took together, laughed, and talked like we were sisters about everything. I will never forget how you claimed me as your sister and how you were there for me when I didn't even want to be in this world. Because of you, I got confidence, and started believing in myself. I also want you to know I was wrong for choosing Edward over you, when you were the one that was there for me when he wasn't during the duration of our marriage. I continue looking at the sign you gave me one year for Christmas that said Best Friends Forever. You stood there for me when no one else did. You are an amazing woman that I love so much. I know I messed up when it came to our relationship, but I do hope when you finish reading this book you will accept my apology. I would love to build another relationship little by little, so you will know I am not that weak person any longer. I am a person that you would be proud of, the person you wanted me to be years ago. A person that you will really love, not that you didn't love me before, but you will love the changes I have made in my life and the person I have became because of them changes. I miss you and I love you, and I miss our trips together and this time we would have a better time because today all I talk about is great things that are happening in my life. Today I am a strong individual, a person that is confident, strong, and a person just like you. I love you Tammy Ann.

Table of Contents

My Dedication	3
Introduction Remembering The Past	5
Chapter 1 My Grill	10
Chapter 2 The Feeling of Numbness Coming Back	13
Chapter 3 The feeling of being lonely	19
Chapter 4 Learning more about Edward	24
Chapter 5 Coming Clean with Edward	29
Chapter 6 Coming back Together so I Thought	33
Chapter 7 Finally telling him my conditions	37
Chapter 8 Getting my answers	40
Chapter 9 Finally moving into our home	44
Chapter 10 The fight on Christmas	49
Chapter 11 The weekend of our marriage	56
Chapter 12 The Ugly Truth	61
Chapter 13 The Honeymoon Night	66
Chapter 14 The First Two Weeks Of Being Married to Edward	71
Chapter 15 More Medical Problems and Bad Habits	75
Chapter 16 Getting Sick of Tired of being Sick and Tired	79
Chapter 17 Being a Better Mother than what I had	83
Chapter 18 Finding Peace In My Storms	88
Chapter 19 Postponing my move	92
Chapter 20 Doing as God wanted Writing my Books of Pain to help others	96
Problems Of Abuse and Statistics	100
DOMESTIC VIOLENCE FACTS	102
SEXUAL ASSAULT AND STALKING	103

Introduction Remembering The Past

I was headed to my grill at three in morning to make breakfast for my customers and I was exhausted. I never got sleep, I worked fifteen hours a day and had huge amount of responsibility. I was trying to keep a business running in the economy that was sluggish then like it is now. My oldest son Justin was in Afghanistan. So, I had that on my mind as well. I prayed that he would be safe. I would come home after being at the grill all day and I would turn on CNN or any other news station that was keeping up on the war in Afghanistan. I would watch to see if anything was happening that might have to do with my son.

My second son, Jordan, was living on the streets. He was doing things that I didn't really approve of. But, because he was my son, I tried hard to be there for him. I didn't want him to go through the same types of struggles that I had gone through in my own life. I tried so hard to be the Mother to my children that I hadn't had as a child while growing up.

I couldn't talk to my Mother about anything in my life when I was a child. My Mother resented me and showed me very little love. Do not get me wrong my Mother was a very hard worker and so was my Father. They gave us what we needed like: clothes, food, and a nice home. But, as a child, I remember sitting at the table for dinner and not being allowed to talk because we were children. But, I remember hearing about their jobs every single night. My Mother and Father worked at the same place.

Looking back, now, as an adult, knowing what a true relationship is, I finally realized my Parents never had one. They only talked about work. My parents never asked any of the children how our day went, what was going on in school, what our favorite color was, our favorite food, or even our favorite number. In reality, our parents did not know us at all.

I tried really hard to know each of these things about my children. I wanted to be a better parent than mine had been. I wanted to know my children, everything about them. And, I wanted to be a parent they felt like they could always talk to. For example, my oldest, Justin, didn't require all the name brand clothes that his younger brother, Jordan, or his younger sister, Meghan, did. Justin always knew what he wanted to do after finishing high school, and that was to join the Navy and he did. The day he left brought back so many bad memories in my life.

When Justin was born, he was premature. He only weighed four pounds and eight ounces. But he was a fighter, even then. However, because he was a premature baby, he often got sick. I knew I had to care of Justin and take him to the Doctors when he was sick, no matter the cost. I was afraid of loosing another child. My parents took my first child, a daughter named Angel, because her biological father told them horrible lies about me, and they believed him.

Justin got really sick when he was just three months old. I had no money or anyway to pay for his doctor's visits and so I went to my father and asked him for help. Instead of helping, he said straight to my face, "Michelle, I didn't make him. You did. So, do whatever you have to and do not bother me again." He knew my situation and understood that I had no way to pay for doctor visits but he didn't care. So, I did what I thought I had to do. I took Justin to the Doctor and wrote several bad checks just to get him the medical attention he needed.

Eventually all of the bad checks caught up with me and I was in trouble and with the law. There was a warrant out for my arrest and when they came and took me to jail, they asked if it would be ok to call my parents to come and take Justin. I immediately said no, but suggested that I could call my brother Joe. My brother Joe was the only one that didn't go to court and testify against me when it came to my first child, Angel. He didn't think it was right that my parents took my daughter away from me. Joe thought they should have helped me instead.

Finally, Joe showed up at the police station and picked up Justin. I cried because I was afraid of loosing another child. While I was being processed the jail officers found out I was pregnant. I had to be transported to Raleigh Central Prison of Safekeeping because they didn't house pregnant women at the local jail. The place was terrible and the cockroaches were so big that they could have carried you off. Each night I stuffed my ears and nose with toilet paper and covered my head with the blanket they issued us so the bugs couldn't crawl over me.

I felt as if those were the six longest months of my life. Not only was I was pregnant with my third child but I had to live with the fact that all three of my children had different biological fathers. My son was with my brother, my first child was with my parents, and I did not know how I was going to take care of the child I was carrying. My life was in a terrible mess.

The entire time I lived at the Safe-house, I never received a letter or had a visit from any of my family. I carried the burden of shame and felt as if no one loved me at all. The night I was finally released I was seven months pregnant and had to hitch hiked from Raleigh, NC to Pink Hill, NC because no one came to pick me up. It took me over five hours to reach my parents house. When I rang the door bell, it was right at midnight. My dad came to the door in his underwear and instead of hugging me, the first thing that came out of his mouth was, "What did you do break out?"

That night was a night I will never forget, as long as I live. The things my parents said to me that night hurt so badly. My dad did let me come in but neither of my parents hugged me nor did they tell me that they loved me. All they did was berated and belittle me. They told me how they thought I was a horrible mother and that I was useless. I told them that I had been released but that I was on probation for two years and that meant that I couldn't leave the State of North Carolina. When I told my parents it didn't even seem to matter to them. They informed me that I would not be allowed to stay at their home. Then I found out that my son Justin was there instead of being at my Brother Joe's home. I was so scared by that point because I was afraid they would try to take him, like they had, Angel. When I asked to see my son they instantly said, "NO" because he was asleep and they didn't want me waking him. I was so hurt, all I wanted was to hold my little boy, and they wouldn't let me.

At this point, my sister Debbie came out of her room. She was also hateful to me and told my parents that if I were allowed to stay that night she would leave and stay at my brother's house. My feelings were badly hurt. All I could do is hold my head down in shame. I wasn't even allowed to take a shower in their home that night. But, that wasn't even the worst part, after finally getting about two hours asleep my Dad woke me up and said let's go and handed me my son. I was so relieved. I held Justin so tight while tears poured down my checks.

When I walked to the bathroom to tell my mother goodbye I received another shock. My first daughter, Angel was in the room with my mother. She started spouting the horrible things my parents had coached her to say to me. I could not believe that at the age of three she had been brainwashed to say such terrible things to me. Angel looked at me and said, "Michelle you are not a good Mother."

Hearing Angel call me Michelle instead of Momma hurt more than words can say. But, hearing her call my Mother, "Momma" made my eyes fill up with tears. I just couldn't understand how my parents could talk so hatefully about me to a three year old little girl, knowing that anything they said to her she would repeat to me. I also could not understand how my Mother would be willing to hurt me after she herself had been hurt by loosing a child of her own. She had my older sister, Carrie, taken away from her because she had an affair and became pregnant with me while she was still married to Carrie's father. I felt like my parents had thrown me away in order to replace me with my own daughter.

In my mind, that is how my Mother got even with me. After that day, we no longer had any type of mother/daughter relationship. My parents continued to coach Angel to hate me and to this day, she is more their child than my own. When my other children Justin, Jordan and Meghan were small, I kept Angel's hatred away from them. I didn't want them to have bitter feelings toward their Grandparents. But, because their grandparents never reached out to them on their own Justin, Jordan and Meghan formed their own opinion about them and it wasn't positive. To this day, my three youngest children do not recognize my parents as their grandparent's.

While Justin was in Afghanistan, my other two children, Jordan and Meghan, helped me in the grill. Jordan was a great cook and Meghan had an awesome personality and was a very good waitress. I also had others working for me, because the grill was open at five in the morning and didn't close until nine pm. So, it was a whole lot of work. I was a hard boss to work for because I wanted everything perfect. Unfortunately, I went through a lot of employees. I found that most people would fire themselves because of their lack of any kind of work ethic. Most of these employees just wanted a paycheck but did not want to work in order to earn a paycheck. One of my biggest mottos is if you have time to lean then you have time to clean. So, many employees didn't care for me to much, but I didn't care. I had regular customers that expected a level of service that I had given them for several years and I refused to compromise that. When many of my regulars drove into the grill's parking lot, I would recognize them and start their breakfast before they could even walk in the door. Many of my customers appreciated that and recognized how hard I worked. These were the same customers that were so amazed by my memory. They couldn't understand how I could remember what they wanted to eat every morning.

My grill sat close to the local high school and so I always had busy mornings. I truly enjoyed cooking for others and although I never really considered myself an awesome cook, I had many repeat customers. They all agreed that I was a good cook even though I sometimes let my past haunt my thoughts. I remember when my first husband, Bob, took a meatloaf that I had accidentally burned and shoved it in my face along with a dirty sock. I had been trying to comfort our sick daughter, Angel, and hadn't been paying close enough attention to dinner.

Being a local girl helped my grill business. Most everyone knew me from either having gone to high school with me or from having grown up in the area. When I was incarcerated at the Safekeeping house for pregnant women, I developed a severe case of OCD. I became obsessed with having things clean and in order. While my children were small, I would vacuum and clean the bathrooms everyday before we would leave the house. And, even though I knew, no one had been home during the day and I would go through the same chores as soon as we got home. I never went to be with one dirty dish or piece of silverware left in my sink. I also obsessed over the laundry. I believe that everything has its place. Organization is the key.

By the time, I was working the grill, I had suffered through several failed marriages, my children were growing up and leaving the house, and I was lonely. Even being around a lot of people did not keep me from being lonely. I seemed to have picked the losers when it came to my husbands. They were either alcoholics or drug addicts and were either mentally, physically, or verbally abusive. At this point in my life, nothing seemed to satisfy me, and I felt like I didn't belong. I tried, unsuccessfully, to kill myself on three different occasions because of all the pain and trauma I had been through.

During my first marriage to Bob, I was continually abused even while I was pregnant with our daughter, Angel. When she was born, I did not know what to do or where to turn to. I tried asking my parents for help but instead of helping, they listened to Bob's lies and went to court and I declared an unfit mother. After the divorce, I was forced to live on the streets for a while. I found shelter in abandoned homes and barns and literally felt like trash. Because of all the heartache, I truly believed that I did not deserve to be happy because I was a whore and trash that needed to be thrown out.

After three failed marriages, I was miserable with myself and miserable with my lot in life. I could not seem to find any good companions. I always seemed to pick the losers. They stayed drunk, were jobless, or were continually physically abusing me. The sad part about it is that I thought I deserved to get beat and verbally abused. Hearing someone, bad mouth you and call you horrible names for so long, you began to believe what they are telling you. To top all of that off, my parents were cruel enough to take my oldest daughter from me and treated me like I couldn't do anything right.

Right after my second child, Justin, was born; I was arrested and put in jail for writing bad checks and skipping out on probation. I always felt their was a shadow following behind me and that I would never break free. Even as a child, I never felt like I fit in. My skin color was a little darker than everyone else's and I grew up in a small but very prejudiced town. When I was in the second grade, I couldn't understand why I was being made fun of. To this day, I am still not sure why I have been persecuted by so many but I am finally beginning to understand that I do not have to please anyone but myself. Working at the grill has allowed me to gain some much needed confidence and helped me realize that I am a tough woman and now I do not hold anything back. If I have something on my mind, I am not afraid to share it.

On the day of the grand opening for my grill, I was so nervous. I was afraid that no one would come because I was the owner. But, to my happy surprise, I was so busy I could barely keep up. Of course, there always has to be one bad apple in the bunch and there was. A wealthy man came in to eat and started to bad mouth my grill. I knew that if I didn't put a stop to him that everyone would try to run me over the same way and I wasn't going to be anyone's stomping ground. So, I calmly and politely walked over to the man and told him to leave my grill and to never return. I made it clear to him that he was not welcome in the grill while I had ownership of it. The town was shocked. They had no idea that I could stand up for myself but I had learned the hard way while in jail that if you didn't stand your ground then the verbal and physical abuse would just continue. I had learned not to be afraid and learned how to speak my mind.

I was making a good living while working in the grill. We were always packed on Thursday, Friday, and Saturday nights when I started having seafood in the evening. The grill was busier that it had ever been with the previous owners. We were usually so packed in the evening that there would be a waiting line. Our business hours were long and grueling. Everyday I was exhausted by the time we would close.

One of the many reasons I opened the grill was so that, hopefully, my mom and I could begin to have some kind of relationship. My mom had always wanted to own her own restaurant. I had tried everything to have a better relationship with her but she continued to hurt me. She had replaced me with my own daughter. She even went so far as to remove all of the pictures of me in her house. There were pictures of my daughter and my siblings but none of me and my other three children. It hurt every time I would have to go to their house for something and I wondered, constantly, if it would ever change.

It seemed to me that my mother always hated me because she got pregnant with me while having an affair. Because of the affair and pregnancy, they declared her an unfit mother and she lost custody of my older sister Carrie. So, as a child, I always felt unloved and unwanted by my own mother. I tried everything I could think of to make her proud and to catch her attention so that maybe she might find some love in her heart for me but it was to no avail.

I always felt like I was the black sheep of my family. Not only did my mother make my life miserable while growing up, she continued to make me miserable by believing my first husband's lies and by taking my daughter away from me. That time in my life was probably the worst and left me with a very low self-esteem. I spent years looking for someone to love me and always found the exact opposite.

Years later when I opened the grill, I thought the relationship with my mother might get better because she had always wanted a restaurant. Again, I was proven wrong. My mother is a very cold, sad, and unloving person. She has no personality to speak of and never shows any kind of affection. When I was a child, I cannot remember her ever smiling or laughing. She treated my younger siblings better than she ever thought about treating me. I hoped when I opened my grill that she might be proud of me and for awhile I truly thought, she was.

The three children I was able to keep with me, Justin, Jordan, and Meghan, did not have any family besides me. My parents would not have anything to do with them and they did not have any contact with their fathers or their families. My children and I have always been close. I tried to make sure that they knew their mother loved them. My heart always ached for my oldest daughter, Angel, and it probably always will but I know I will never have any kind of relationship with her because of the poison my parents have fed her. They have taught my own daughter to hate me and that hurts.

When the business at my grill started to pick up, my mother asked if she could come and help out. I agreed because I thought it would be a good way for us to spend some time together and maybe it would help our relationship. Unfortunately, that didn't happen. She would come to the grill and would man the register and sit, smoke, and I would let her because I truly wanted to have her in my life. I even hired my sister Debbie and paid my mother and sister really well even though they only did a quarter of the work I asked them to do. My sister began to resent me because she thought my mother and I were having a closer relationship than she had with our mother.

They actually began to think that the grill belonged to them and not me. I did not correct this thinking because I was just happy to have some of my family around me and wanted so badly to be a part of their lives.

I would occasionally get to see my oldest daughter Angel when she would come to the grill to see my mom or sister. Even though she was grown it was nice to see her and it always made me happy. My regular customers soon figured out that she belonged to me because she is the spitting image of me. Out of all four of my children, Angel looks the most like me. Unfortunately, my other three children do not like their half sister because she has been raised by my parents and brainwashed to hate us all. They also knew that the only time Angel would ever contact me of her own accord was when she needed money.

Chapter 1 My Grill

While I had the grill open, I went through a lot of employees. I believed that if you had time to lean you had time to clean and not everyone liked that rule. Most of my employee's would rather eat my food than work for their paychecks. They liked to sit and not take care of things that needed to be taken care of. I eventually had to put security cameras in the grill because I had employees stealing from me. There were also other things happening that should not have been happening. I was also concerned for my safety when opening and closing the restaurant on my own.

During this time, I bought a new house for me and my children. So, in between taking care of the grill and coming home to paint, unpack, and/or clean I became very tired. I also grew more and more lonely. Even though people everyday surrounded me, it was not the same as having someone to come home to or talk to about things when I needed someone. I had customers that tried to fix me up with people, I was even asked out by a few of my customers, but they were all either married, wanted to be friends with benefits, or they were just not my type. It was hard to really accept anyone's invitations because I had had so many failed marriages that I did not feel like I was worthy of anyone's love. I kept my past in the forefront of my mind constantly. I would also remember how my own family treated me and I knew that I did not want to be a part of something like that.

Eventually one of the girls that worked for me at the grill started talking about an online website that would allow you find single people around your area that was interested in dating. It was called singles.net. So, one afternoon when I got home from a long day at work, I logged onto my computer and registered for my free profile. I soon realized that I was back in the same rut even online because of my past. I pretended to be someone I wasn't because it was easier than being me. I became a really good actress and liar. Throughout my life I have visited with counselors to try and help me move on from my past but I never seem to be able to leave it all behind me. My depression got deeper as my children started to leave home and I realized all I had left was the grill. By the time, I had the grill for a good while my parents started treating me like they were actually proud of me. They would even bring company by the grill to show it off to their friends. My father even wrote on a napkin that he was proud of me. I cherished that napkin. I hung it up on my refrigerator and when I would get down on myself, I would go over and read it.

Before I owned the grill, I had been so desperate to have my family in my life that I had lied to my parents, telling them that I was so sick that I was dying. I wanted to have a family like something from "The Little House on the Prairie" or "The Walton's." My three youngest children and I did have somewhat of this type of family unit. We had a motto that hung on the fridge while they were growing up that read: "We're tough, We're strong, and We always Stick together No matter What." My kids have always been there for me even when I was making mistakes because I have always been there for them. They understand that I did not have an easy childhood and so they have always rallied around me when I have needed it. The three of them have never had any kind of relationship with my family because my family has never offered to be a part of their lives. My kids have formed their own opinions about my family from the way they have treated me.

When my kids were little I tried to make sure they interacted with their grandparents but what they remember from those times is that they were belittled and punished by people that did not love them. When my daughter Meghan was about five years old we were at my parents house for a holiday and she was playing with some of my mother's knick knacks she had all over the house. Meghan accidentally broke a small ceramic baby duck and my mother instantly picked her up and spanked her without even asking me. My sons were also playing, that same year, with their cousin Steven, my sister Debbie's son. The boys were jumping on one of the beds because kids will do that sometimes especially when they get bored. My mother went to tell them to stop, was hateful to my two sons, and asked my nephew, nicely, to stop what he was doing. The kids were ready to go home when it was time and when we left they all three told me "they are mean people Momma and we do not like them." Tears streamed down my face as we drove away because my children couldn't understand how my family could be so mean. It wasn't long after we left when my oldest son Justin asked "Momma do we ever have to go back there again?" I quietly answered him with a "No."

As they were growing and forming their own opinions of my family they would get frustrated with me because I would continually try to have some kind of relationship with my family. My kids could not understand why I would even try after all; they had done to me and put me through. I tried to explain to them it was because no matter what I loved them and they were my family. It seemed like I was always defending my parents to my children and my children to my parents. I would sometimes feel like a yoyo bouncing between the two.

Even while my mom and sister worked at the grill, my children barely tolerated their presence and only did for me. They knew that I wanted to have some kind of relationship with my family and so they would hold their tongues and tried their best not to say anything negative to them. I lived for the days that Angel would visit the grill. Just catching a glimpse of her made me happy. I had always felt like their was a hole in my heart when she was taken away by my parents and so when I was able to get a picture of her or see her it always seemed to make me feel better.

To this day, I do not know if my parents really understand how much their actions affected me and my life. If they had chosen to help me become a better and more responsible mother, I truly believe my life would have been different. Their deception hurt me more than I can ever admit. It was extremely painful to have to listen to your own parents talk so hatefully about you to a courtroom full of people that do not even know you. Even worse was when that courtroom decided to believe my parents that had lied instead of me, someone that was just trying to make it as a single mother.

The only people that I felt really ever loved me were my children Justin, Jordan, and Meghan. My parents never took us to church and so I did not know God. I walked around for most of my life thinking that I was unworthy of love. I assumed that if your own family did not love you then how complete strangers could be expected to love you.

When I opened the grill, I had just moved back to the area where I had grown up after three failed marriages. I had hope that once people got to know me again, they would realize that I was a good person and for awhile it seemed to be working. Even my parents seemed proud of me for awhile. I knew that one of my mom's biggest dreams had always been to open her own restaurant and so that was one of the major reasons I opened the grill. I really thought it would be something for her to be proud of me and would give her a way to feel like she was fulfilling a dream as well.

My biggest dream had not been to open a restaurant; it was to be a writer. Growing up I filled journal after journal with my life story as well as stories I would make up. Even after loosing my first child, journaling seemed to help me with her loss. There were many times during my life that I would just write instead of talking. I have gone back through many of my journals from some of the hardest places in my life and there have been times when I have believed what my family has always told me. That I was nothing. I know now that just is not true but for a long time I believed it.

For a long time I just pretended to be happy with myself. I would wake up every morning, drive to the restaurant, and work, and then go home alone and unhappy. I learned to bottle things inside of me. Too many times in my life I had people use my weaknesses against me and I refused to have that happen anymore and so I showed everyone on the outside what they expected to see. There were so many times when my family used my failed marriages, my jail time, or loosing my first child against me. They would verbally abuse me, most of the time in order to get whatever they wanted from me. I would usually cave to their wishes because I didn't want to argue or hear their criticisms any longer.

I eventually learned not to share anything about my past with anyone. If they didn't have the information then they couldn't use it against me. I began to lie about my past so that I wouldn't have to see the pity or condemnation in others eyes. The only people I could be completely honest with were my children. I would tell them everything and I trusted them completely. If they ever had questions about me or my life, I would be honest and upfront with them. I tried to teach them by example so that they would do the same with me. They were the only ones that ever saw me cry or ever held me while I was depressed. My children loved me and I them.

When I was diagnosed with MS, I knew no one in my family besides my brother Joe would help me. My children were the ones that helped me the most when I would have a bad episode and could not do for myself. Justin would cook, Meghan would help me bathe, and Justin would help the others keep the house clean the way I would have done had I been able to.

Chapter 2 The Feeling of Numbness Coming Back

My children understood me when no one else ever did. They adored and loved me so very much. When I hurt, they also hurt because of their love for me. They are so amazing in every single way. My kids were my warriors and they knew that their mother loved them unconditionally. Especially, my oldest son Justin he was my protector and even when I was wrong he would stand behind me in any way possible. They all hated it when I cried, and hated watching me get hurt over and over again especially by my own family.

So, when they saw me open the grill and it became almost an over night hit, my kids were so excited for their mom. The rush was not limited to just breakfast, but also included lunch and dinner as well. My son Jordan couldn't believe how my customers acted as if they cared so much for me and he saw his Mom really charm these people with a much different personality than he had ever seen. I had always been really outgoing even as a child and in high school, I always was called a social butterfly, but things changed after I graduated, got married, and had my first child.

Business was really going very well until I let my Mother and my sister Debbie get involved in helping me run the grill. By the time I brought my Mother and sister Debbie into the grill, I had already had formed a customer base relationship and had lots of regulars and I knew them by name. Not long after their arrival, I began to notice that many of my regular customers were not returning. I kept asking myself what was going on and came to the conclusion that it was because of the economy and high gas prices. I soon had to down size my employees. When I had to do that, it created more work for me. I was getting extremely tired. So, as my customers dwindled it gave me more responsibility. I now had the job of cleaning, shopping, ordering, doing payroll, and cooking all by myself. The relationships I had built with my customers were dropping because I wasn't able to connect with them on a personal level like I had been able to previously.

Finally, one of my customers came to me and told me that they had witnessed my Mother blow her nose in the kitchen area, and then fix someone's plate without even washing her hands. This was during the time when I still had lots of regulars. Now that I had so few I, was forced to bring this to my Mother's attention. Instead of apologizing, she said to me, "Michelle, I take this shit from your Father and I will not take it from you." She then slammed the towel she had in her hands down onto the floor and walked out. I knew what was happening, the same Vanessa I remember from when I was a child was coming out. I began to cry again not only because of her actions and the way she felt about me but also because she had humiliated me in my own establishment.

That night I was very sad and depressed while headed home and I was still very lonely. Every evening I would check my e-mail to see if I had received any new e-mail from the dating site I had joined. To my amazement, that evening, I had several e-mails. But, there was one I paid particular attention to. It was from a man named Edward. I knew, Edward and had known him since I we were both eleven years old. We had worked together in tobacco and had also gone to high school together. When I opened the email from Edward, all it said was, "Hi." It made me curious. I went to bed wondering about Edward. I was curious to know if he still remembered me, what he had been up to since last I saw him, and what he was doing now. I did not even return his email I was still trying to remember what I knew about him. It felt strange to think about someone I had known since I was eleven.

Since my sister Debbie was the nosey one in the family, I called her and asked her all sorts of questions about him. The next day, she told me he was never married and he was forty three, he had his own place, and never had any children. She also said that he was an electrician, and liked to drink a little beer and liquor. I liked all of it but the drinking part. Debbie also said he was tight with the dollar. But, by having the grill, I had also learned to be tight with my money as well, so I respected that a great deal. That wasn't something that bothered me. Edward was so handsome to me; he had gorgeous lips, with very dark hair and beautiful eyes. Edward also had a very square chin, which was so handsome with a mustache and a goatee.

The one thing that I did notice about him was that he never smiled or even spoke to anyone. Edward even scared my waitress's to the point they didn't even want to wait on him. He acted like he had absolutely no personality and seemed to be a very dry person. For a while, Edward reminded me of my own Mother. The next morning after receiving his e-mail, he didn't come to the grill and so I was afraid that maybe he had accidentally e-mailed the wrong girl, or made a mistake, I always assumed the worst. I never thought I was good enough for anyone especially after so many failed marriages.

I never told anyone about my past and never even married a man or even dated anyone ever in this area before in my life since high school. But, somehow, this small town always knew everything about everyone. I always pretended I was happy when I was completely miserable. All I had positive in my life was my children; they made me happy, I was so very proud of Justin for the man he had become. I had always told Justin he was a much better man at eighteen than his real dad was at forty. Justin had character, he had pride, and most important he had a heart like you wouldn't believe. Justin reminded me of myself always a person that wanted to please everyone, even when I couldn't afford to please people.

When Justin was small, I forced adult problems onto his shoulders when I should have just let him be a child. He was the man of the house; he protected me and his younger siblings. Justin was my hero in so many ways and such a precious child. My son stood behind me whether or not if I was right or wrong and I have to say I have made some lousy choices.
Jordan was my comedian, a laid back young man, reminded me of myself also when I was just a little girl until I found out the truth about my parents and how hard my Mother had made my heart become. It was such a miserable feeling knowing how my own Mother had such bitter feelings towards me.

I tried really hard to not display that anger to my children but at times, I did, especially the times they wouldn't listen to me. Jordan was my social butterfly. He always had a lot of friends. I had never seen the importance of having so many friends because during my life my friends and family only ever hurt me. So, as an adult I couldn't understand why Jordan wanted to have so many friends, however, I tried really hard to allow him to be himself. Jordan was also the child that really tried to push every button that I had as well. It was nothing for us to have ten to twelve boys in my house every single weekend because Jordan made friends so easily. I remember making friends easily but because of my horrible home life I never wanted my friends to come to my home, Jordan was also a child that would continue asking if he could do something even after he had already been told NO. He would keep asking until I would get exhausted and would cave.

I never realized what a little monster I was creating till one day while Jordan was still in his senior year of high school I received a phone call from the school. To my surprise, he was skipping classes. Jordan was so smart that he made great grades without even bringing home books; he was just that gifted. He and Justin both never had to study. Well, at that moment I knew he was too big to spank so I decided I would do something he would not like and teach him a serious lesson. I called my head cook at the grill and asked her if she could handle the grill for the day and she agreed that she could. So, the following morning when Jordan left to go to the school, I followed him. Little did he know he had a surprise coming to him? When I got to his school, I was dressed in my pajamas, hair was a mess, and I had no make up. I made my way to his first period class and waited. As the first bell rang, I didn't see Jordan come into the classroom, so I walked out of the class into the hallway and I saw him slowly making his way down the hall towards his class. As soon as he saw me, he immediately changed his facial expressions. Jordan immediately asked me, "Mom why are you here?" I replied, "Jordan since you cannot seem to get yourself to class I will be here all day to make sure you do not miss anything." Jordan begged and pleaded with me to go home. He said he would be so embarrassed. I explained to him, "son I am here because I love you and you may not understand why now, but you will when you get older." Jordan cried and pleaded with me to go home. But, I refused. I followed him all day and went to every class with him. After that day, he never missed school again. That was all it took for Jordan to understand I was not playing. Jordan finished and graduated from high school and then got a job to learn how to be an electrician. I was so proud of him. Sometimes he would still help me when he could in the grill.

Meghan was a child that had such an imagination, a tender heart and was so innocent. I never had to spank her, all I had to do was just raise my voice, and she would cry. Meghan looked a lot like me. We shared a lot of the same features but it was still nothing compared to how my first daughter Angel and I looked so much alike. So, I suppose I was more lenient on her. Meghan worked at the grill also along with Jordan and they were awesome. I taught my children at a very young age that you had to work and have values because money did not come easily. Justin was already in the military in the USN but when he came home to visit, he would also work in the grill. I was so proud of my all of my children and I loved them all dearly.

Having all the responsibility of being a single Mom and running a business still left me lonely. I often thought about Edward and wondered why he had not been in the grill for a while. Then one day to my surprise he showed up at the grill and since my waitress's didn't like waiting on him because of his personality, I took it upon myself to help him. I went over and asked him, "Where have you been?" He replied that he had been sick with bronchitis. I then replied that I had missed seeing him.

At that point, we exchanged phone numbers. The weird thing was the last four digits of his phone number were 0611 and mine was 0911. I thought that was a sign from God. I always tried to do what God wanted me to do. Even though I had not grown up with God, I believed He was there and so, I wanted to believe it was a sign. So, the rest of the day at the grill I was very happy, thinking God had finally answered my prayers and brought me someone I could share my life with.

We looked alike, and I thought we could really make something great happen. Especially him having never being married and also not having any children, I knew that was blessings because the last thing I wanted to do was help raise more children when my children were almost grown. I thought how perfect, and in my mind, I actually thought this was a sign from God.

The day was winding down at the grill and even though I knew that after closing the grill I still had bank deposits to make, I also had to go to the grocery store for our supplies for the next day, but for some strange reason I had more energy, than I had had in months. I knew that was because of Edward. After giving him my number, I just knew he would call me that night when I got home from work. So, finally after getting home the first thing I did was check my answering machine. I was disappointed when I saw nothing from him but I didn't worry because I just knew he would call. Then I checked my e-mail, thinking he might have sent me something that way, but again nothing.

That's when I began to worry. Then as usual terrible thoughts would come rushing back in my head. Why would a guy like Edward want a girl like me? A girl that's been to jail, a girl that has slept with men just to survive, and a girl that had already had so many failed marriages. Did he find out all this stuff? I wondered and I worried and the more I did this the worse my mood got. So, I finally decided to go make dinner for Meghan, Jordan and myself. After we ate, I cleaned the kitchen up and then I went and took a shower because I still smelled like grease from the grill and felt dirty.

After that, I worked on my book work from the grill and wrote down items that the grill needed from my main supplier. Still while I was doing this, I was waiting for a phone call from Edward but the phone never rang. I have always been able to work while thinking about other things as well. I eventually remembered something my Aunt had told me a long time ago when I lived in Georgia. She said, "Michelle, you do not have to tell anyone about your past. When you do, they always have a way to bring it up to you when it is convenient for them and make you feel even more horrible than you do already." That always stuck with me and the more I thought about that while doing my work for the grill I eventually thought that it was probably best that Edward didn't call. In my head I said to myself, I do not even understand things how in the world would a sane person understand so I put them thoughts of Edward to rest. I figured it was for the best, and it made me very sad. Soon after finishing my book work for the grill, and watching CNN and other news networks, just to see about the war in Afghanistan where my son Justin was, I soon thought I better get to bed because of having to get up so early. I only got about three to four hours asleep a night.

Just about the time I got to sleep, my phone rang and woke me up. I immediately looked at the clock and realized it was after eleven pm. I had no clue who might be calling because everyone knew that after about nine thirty, I was in the bed. I had to get up very early every morning and so I went to bed early every night. When I answered the phone, I wasn't very polite. With my not so polite voice I said, "Hello? Who is this?" There was a long pause and so I repeated myself. Then to my surprise, I heard Edward say his name. I asked him, "What do you want? You know I have to get up early in the morning so why are you calling me so late?" Edward did not even explain. All he asked was if I would like to have some company? I replied NO in a very firm voice. It hurt my feelings because I felt like all he wanted was one thing and I was not willing to give him that. Before I hung the phone up, I told Edward to never call me this late again.

Well, after getting off the phone I thought to myself that I would probably never hear from Edward again because of the way I handled the phone call. But, I reminded myself that I was not a whore, that I would not be treated as such, and that I refused to put myself in that type of situation again. So, I was finally able to sleep but I didn't rest well at all that night. Before I knew it, the alarm was going off. At that moment I realized that I not only hated my alarm clock but that I hated that clock and in reality I hated the grill.

The main reason I opened the grill was for my Momma. I rarely saw her or my sister Debbie and so I opened the grill hoping that we could build a family relationship the way it should have been from the start. But, on that particular morning, I wasn't in the best of moods because I knew I probably would never hear from Edward again. So, after getting to the grill, I started my daily routine. I worked on prepping everything for the breakfast and lunch rushes never once thinking about Edward. When I opened the grill and turned my open sign on, I then allowed myself a brief thought for Edward. I wondered if he would show up that morning but alas, he did not. So, because Edward did not come by the grill it made for an extremely long and lonely day for me. It just so happened to be a Thursday and I knew that my day would be a never ending one because we were open in the evenings on Thursday, Friday, and Saturday. I bemoaned the fact that I would have to be at the grill until ten that evening. Those three days were always the longest and it always made me so very tired. I closed the grill at three on the days that we had a dinner service in order to prepare for the evening rush. I had to be much focused and with help with my children, we always made it.

I could not have ever made the grill work without my kids because I knew deep down that they were the only ones that actually cared about me and my dreams. My children have had to watch me go through some horrible times in my life but they were always there for me, no matter what. There where many times when we would return home late at night and they would rub my legs and feet because I was in so much pain due to my MS. Bless their hearts, I was always in pain in more than one way and I tried really hard to hide it from my kids, but somehow they always knew.

That night after closing the grill, I realized that we had had an awesome day at the grill and that I had not even had time to even think about Edward. However, I did decide to call him back that evening when I returned home to apologize for the way I had treated him when he phoned the night before. I was so nervous when I made that phone call. I was not even sure whether or not he would even talk to me, and if he did what we would even talk about. However, I dialed the number and it rang and rang. I was about to give up on him when he finally he answered. It was late and I was afraid that he might have been asleep. So, when he answered I said hello and asked him what he was doing? He replied that he was outside grilling some food. I was trying to be nice and so I asked if he had enough for two. His instant reply was a resounding NO.

At that point, I got the feeling that he really did not want to talk to me any longer. So, I told him that I had thrown a party for my employee's the week before and had a lot of alcohol left over from the party. I explained to him that I did not drink alcohol but that if he were interested in having any of it he was welcome to come by and pick it up. He immediately said he would be interested.

    To my surprise, we only lived about ten minutes apart. So, he said he would come by and collect the left over alcohol as soon as he finished eating his dinner. Edward didn't come into the house because I had all the left over alcohol on my back porch. When he came to collect it, I assumed he would just take some of it but to my surprise, he took all of it. But I knew it would go to waste if I didn't give it to someone, and because my sister Debbie had informed me that he liked to drink I thought it might be a good way to get into his good graces. I really assumed that the alcohol would last him a good long time.

    When he came to retrieve the alcohol, he was pleasant and friendly. Edward was very good looking and was exactly everything I thought I wanted and needed in a man. So, the next day when I opened the grill and he came in, thought it must be God's will. Edward always had the exact money for whatever he ordered. I thought that was a little strange but I really didn't give it much thought at that time. When he left that day, I told my employees that I liked him. To my surprise, they couldn't believe it and even one particular employee said to me, "Michelle he is all wrong for you." I paid her no mind because I thought God was giving me signs that Edward was the right one for me. I really didn't care what others thought.

    The only hang up I had with Edward was his drinking. When I asked him about it he told me that he only drank a little and so that is what I believed. Like most woman, I thought I could change the man. I continued to try to get to know him more. After a while he would come into the grill and order his food and I would no longer even charge him Once again, I was trying to please everyone else but myself. I watched him realize what I was doing for him and he really seemed to like what I was doing for him. So, one morning I asked him if he would like to go out with me on Sunday. I told him that I would have my niece and nephew with me but that we would go out to eat and would then catch a movie. To my pleasant surprise, he said yes.

    When he would come over to visit me at my house, he very rarely drank and I was glad of that because there were often time that my niece and nephew were with me. I thought that his drinking was something I could accept and learn to live with. When Sunday rolled around I went and picked up my niece and nephew early so that we could wait at my house for Edward and then we would all be ready to go. Later in our relationship, if we ever had to go somewhere we would always have to take my vehicle because his two cars were not reliable or safe to drive any sort of distance. So, that first evening, I had agreed to drive us on our date. My niece, nephew, and I were all waiting impatiently for Edward to arrive and when it came to be past time for him to arrive I told them that if he didn't show up in the next few minutes we would leave with out him. About five minutes later, Edward finally makes an appearance but could tell from the look on his face that he was not happy about having my niece and nephew along on our first date. I was never really sure whether it was because of the kids or whether he was afraid, they might cut into his drinking time.

    When we got to the mall where the movie theater was located, my nephew and niece were getting excited because they really wanted to see the movie and they really liked that I was getting to spend some time with them. I missed out on a lot in their lives because I was always working. So, when we parked and got out of the car to head inside, my niece took Edward's hand and my hand and then put our hands together. I felt like a teenager and loved it; however I didn't get the same feeling or reaction from Edward.

    When we made our way to the window to pick up our movie theater tickets, I noticed that Edward never made a move or offered to pay for the tickets. So, I got the money out of my purse and paid for the movie for all of us. Then we moved inside to the snack bar, again, he never even acted like he might offer to pay for the snacks. I was forced to buy for all of us. Once we were seated in the theater, my niece made sure we were sitting next to each other and also made sure we were holding hands, I was almost immediately ready to leave because Edward was acting like he was not having a good time at all. When the movie was over, we left and my niece and nephew decided that they want to go and eat Mexican food for dinner. I agreed and drove us to a nice Mexican restaurant.

This time I thought for sure, that Edward would offer to pay for our dinner since I had paid for the movie and snacks. When the waiter came to take our drink order, Edward instantly ordered a margarita. I was very disappointed because I had my underage niece and nephew with us. I didn't say anything, but my mind was racing. I kept wondering why he would order alcohol while on a date with me and my niece and nephew. When our dinner came, Edward ordered another margarita. By this time, I was furious. It made me rethink what my sister Debbie had told me about him liking to drink. Maybe he had more of a problem than even she knew. Finally we finished eating and were getting ready to leave; my niece and nephew went out front to wait for us and to my surprise Edward went with them without offering to help me pay for dinner. As per usual, I just sucked it up and didn't say a word because at the time I still believed that I did not deserve anything better. I didn't want to get serious with anyone because of my past and knowing how people would respond especially after being married so many times as I have. So on the way home I was really quite, I had all sorts of thoughts running in my head, and wondering what was going on.

What Edward didn't understand about me then was that my family means everything to me because most of my life I didn't have any type of normal relationship with my family except for my children. I did everything I could to have a relationship with my family. I turned my cheeks more than once for them just like Jesus told us to do in the bible. Edward had a family but from my understanding, he never contacted them except for holidays. I didn't really understand how he could be so far removed from his own family but I didn't feel it was my place to pry.

So, on our way to the movies the kids had drilled Edward all sorts of questions that young children ask everyone they meet. I am sure Edward was very uncomfortable, because some of the questions they asked him also embarrassed me. I finally had to tell my niece to stop because she was the main one asking questions. I suggested that we just let Edward be and told her that we should just relax and try to have a fun time together. So, for a little while she remained silent, but she was a lot like her Aunt Michelle, was full of questions, thoughts, and paid attention to everything.

When we were on our way to take my niece and nephew home, Edward suggested that he would like to spend some time with me. I thought to myself that maybe that was what we needed, so I agreed. But, at the same time, I was wondering why he would want to spend time with me. Especially after the way he had treated me during the movie, and then again at dinner. Edward was very quite on the way home. He barely spoke at all and when he did was not friendly at all with my niece and nephew. I was not happy about that turn of events at all.

All I could think of was why he would want to spend time with me. Was it because he thought I had a huge amount of money or he was looking for a one night stand? Either way I didn't like where I was afraid this might go. However, I knew that I would some times jump to the wrong conclusions. So, I thought I would give him the benefit of the doubt and hear what he might have to say.

Chapter 3 The feeling of being lonely

After dropping off my niece and nephew, Edward asked me to stop at the store so he could get some cigarettes and some beer. I didn't want to stop, but I did. Edward actually went in, picked up, and paid for his beer and cigarettes. When he came out, I assumed he would be bringing a six pack but he came out with a twelve pack. I was shocked, but I also knew I liked him and that he made me laugh. I knew that I liked having an adult to talk to, so I tried really hard to do things to make him like me.

But, at the same time, I remembered growing up with an alcoholic father and I knew I didn't like the idea of going through any of that again. I had never been much of a drinker however I did smoke marijuana from time to time. When I was diagnosed with MS, my Neurologists told me that by smoking marijuana it would help relieve some of the pain that I suffered through most days. I felt like I couldn't judge Edward because I knew that smoking marijuana was illegal even though I had had a doctor tell me to do so.

When we finally arrived back at my house, we decided to sit on the couch and watch another movie. I wanted to feel like I was doing everything I could to fit in with him so I asked him to share a beer with me. Then I told him what my doctor had told me about the marijuana. To my surprise he said that he also smoked but for different reasons. So, we sat on my couch drinking and smoking marijuana. Eventually one thing led to another and we ended up in bed together.

Afterwards, Edward began to cry, I never asked why but maybe I should have. It made me feel like maybe I had done something wrong. Needless to say, he spent the night with me because I couldn't ask him to leave after he cried. The next morning I left early in order to open the grill. I had strange thoughts and feelings going on inside my head that day. Some of them were good and some were bad but most of them centered on the thought that I would never allow this type of situation into my life again.

I didn't know how I was going to tell Edward my past. I was unsure of Edward's feeling toward me. What I also didn't know but found out later was that Edward had tried to date me years before but my Father had run him off. He also told me later that he had recognized me in a store several years later and had attempted to speak to me but I had not even given him a second glance. All I knew for sure was that I came into any relationship with a lot of baggage. I had four children all fathered by different men. I had one child that I had lost custody of because my parents were more concerned with the lies they heard than they were about me and what I might need. How was I supposed to explain the strange and broken relationship I had with my parents because of them taking away my daughter and accusing me of sleeping with black men and doing cocaine. Then I began to contemplate how I would ever explain my criminal record to Edward. I had a feeling that if I divulged everything about me and my past, Edward would leave. I understood that he was extremely concerned with money because that is all he ever talked about with me. I think Edward thought I had a lot of money. I didn't correct or deny his assumptions.

During the time Edward and I were just growing into our relationship, I found out later that he was digging around in my past, trying his best to find things to use against me. At my lowest points, I would do my best to make me look better to others so I began to stretch the truth to Edward. I pretended that I had lots of money, property, and I that didn't need anyone in my life. But, in reality, I did need someone. I needed and wanted someone to love me, help me, and to be there for me. Most of the time, I hardly ever had enough money to pay my home bills and the grill's bills. However, it always seemed like my past always came back and haunted me.

In 2001, I found out I had MS. That is when I lost everything. My good paying job was gone where I had been making a large amount of money every month. I had been driving a BMW and was finally living the American dream. But, when I got sick and could no longer work, I lost everything. I had to file for bankruptcy. I owned twelve acres of land, lived in a five bedroom house with three bathrooms, and had finally been able to do things with my children that I hadn't ever been able to afford before.

How would I be able to tell Edward all of that without being judged, as I have been all my life? It took me a long seven years to pay my bankruptcy off and finally get enough money together to purchase the grill. I had hoped that my family would finally step up and not only help me with the grill but would allow me to be a part of their lives because of the grill.

After purchasing the grill and getting it up and running, I was finally able to start paying my own bills again. The grill was bringing enough revenue that I was no longer falling behind. However, just like most Americans I still lived month to month. I also had three teenagers still living at home and they required lots of money to keep them fed, clothed, and in their extra curricular activities especially in the last year of high school.

I never asked Edward for any kind of financial help. But, as time went by and our relationship lasted, I began to notice that he was showing up later and later at my house after I got off work. Little did I know Edward had paid someone to do a back ground check on me? And then he spent the remainder of his time asking his friends what they knew about me. When Edward got the results of the back ground check, it showed where I had written bad checks all those years ago when I was first diagnosed with MS and my kids were small.

Then Edward started asking me questions about whether or not I knew this person or that person. Because I am bad at names and faces I would always tell him no even if I did know them. Edward would then call me a liar. He usually did this while he was drinking. Edward was always a negative person and reminded me so much of my Mother. Edward was always telling me that he wanted an independent woman, so if I ever needed help I would never ask for anything. I would always go to my best friend, Tammy Ann.

Tammy Ann and I became friends when she started working for me at the grill. We quickly formed a bond and I was able to tell her everything about me and my life and never felt like she was judging me. She helped me and was someone I could always talk to about anything and everything. Tammy Ann and myself spent lots of time together, because her husband Brent was a truck driver and he was gone during the week.

Tammy Ann had a heart of gold and she knew how I could never get a home on my own because of my credit, and she knew I was renting which in her mind and in mine it was like throwing money right out the window. So, Tammy Ann spoke to her cousin who owned a home right next door to her home and asked her cousin if I could do a rent to own. Because of Tammy Ann and the recommendation she gave me, her cousin agreed. When she told me I was so excited. Because of her, I was able to buy my own home and I worked hard fixing up the inside of the house so that it would be just like I wanted it. The best thing about my new home was that I was living right next door to my very best friend.

I was finally able to get back on my feet again after all of those years being down in the dumps. My new home would have been paid for in just four years if it hadn't been for Edward. Edward hated my house because Tammy Ann lived next door. For some reason Edward did not like her, her husband, or even her children at all. They had never done anything to Edward except to be friendly. During this time, I had not shared any of my concerns with Tammy Ann because I wanted her to like Edward.

However, Tammy Ann knew something wasn't right between Edward and me but she never said a word. She loved me and my children but she also knew I wasn't happy either. Tammy Ann knew I was settling because I thought that I didn't deserve anyone better. Because she loved me and my children, she stuck by me just like a best friend should. But, she still didn't like how I was being treated and she could see how Edward was using me. Tammy Ann tried to tell me that he was no good but I just knew that because of my past I did not deserve any better. It was as if I always had this demon whispering in my ear telling, me I was no good.

One afternoon Edward came to the house as usual and he asked me if I knew this person that both he and I had gone to school with. I said the name sounded familiar but that I did not remember him. When I told him that I didn't remember this person, he looked at me like I had grown five sets of eyes. I didn't understand what this person had to do with anything at that point. The next day Edward asked me to go to his house and get his mail out of his mailbox. He had never asked me to do that during our entire relationship so I agreed that I would go over and do it for him, still trying to please him. I had planned to secretly go over to Edward's home anyway because I knew that his yard had not been mowed and I had just finished mowing mine so I planned to go and mow his yard for him. This just gave me another excuse to go by his house. I wanted to surprise him by mowing his yard.

The only difference between his yard and my own was that I had a riding mower and he only had a pushed mower. If you have ever been to North Carolina in October, you know that it is still extremely hot. It took everything I had to mow his yard with his push mower. After finishing mowing his yard and even doing the weed eating in his ditches, I realized that I did not have a key to go into the his home. I really need to go to the bathroom so I was forced to go outside in the woods. Then I needed a drink of water and was forced to use the water hose.

After finishing the yard, I remembered to get the mail. So, after getting the mail, I called him and told him what he had received. However, there was one particular letter that had no return address on it so I couldn't tell him what it was or whom it was from, so he told me to open it. When I opened it, I got the shock of a lifetime. It was a background check on me. I just sat there in his driveway crying, crying, and never said a word to him until he showed up at my house sometime later. By then, I was so mad that I was seeing red. I wondered how he could have done that to me. Then I asked myself why he would have done that to me.

I immediately called my best friend Tammy Ann and told her what I had found. She was shocked as well. Neither of us could believe it. Tammy Ann quickly told me to get rid of Edward and to never look back. She said to me, "Michelle it seems like he wants to know all about you and your past but he will not even share one detail of his past life since high school with you." She was absolutely right. I believe she was as angry as I was because she was the one friend that knew everything about me and knew my demons, and knew how hard I had worked to make my wrongs right. All I did was take care of my responsibilities, my children, and my grill, and worked in my yard and all I got was used.

My best friend Tammy Ann wasn't very crazy about my family either because she was looking in from the outside. I was too close to the situation and she could see me trying so hard to gain their love that she soon realized they would never return openly expect when it suited their needs. My family never came to visit me, nor did they call me, or even asked about their grandchildren and she could not understand how a family could be so cold. But they all expected to eat at my grill for free just like Edward did.

The night Edward came over to my house and of course, I wasn't my usual self, I gave him the cold shoulder. In reality, I didn't even want him to be there. I was also getting to the point that I hated his drinking, but my demons told me I didn't deserve any better, and I believed that. My Father actually told me that if I messed this relationship up with Edward then he would, "kick my ass." Those were his exact words.

Not realizing what Edward was doing to me or even caring how Edward was sponging off of me. Everything was always my fault, and I was reminded of that daily no matter how many years ago it may have happened. To my parents and, I assumed, the people in the community I was nothing but trash. But, that was not true whatsoever; the community actually liked me a lot. Some of the rumors I heard were true but most were lies spread by my own family. I hung my head in shame most of my life. It started the day my parents took my first child, Angel, when I was only nineteen.

So when Edward came home, I just couldn't even bare to look at him. I went outside and sat on the porch swing while I though about everything. Eventually Edward came out to where I was and of coarse he had a beer in his hand. That was what started a horrible argument. He had learned everything about me: losing Angel, having to file for bankruptcy, the bad checks, jail, and even the lies I had told about having things that I didn't really have. Then he learned that I had been forced to sleep with different individuals when my children were small just to put food on the table for them.

Edward for sure made me feel like he was so much better than I was. It hurt me so badly and I cried so hard till I was totally sick to my stomach, Edward never once tried to make things better, he just made things worse. The worst part was the fact that I was at my own home. I eventually realized this and told Edward that he had to leave and then asked him politely not to come back. I walked inside and locked the door.

When I got inside the house, I called my best friend Tammy Ann, she, and I looked out our neighboring windows to see if Edward had heeded my advice and left. But, he hadn't. Edward just remained sitting on the porch swing and refused to leave. Tammy Ann and I stayed on the phone together for at least three hours watching Edward go back and forth to his truck and get beer after beer and then he would walk back to my porch swing.

Finally, she asked me what his problem was. I said I do not know but I do not need this, she said you sure do not. She said Michelle you need to go out there and tell him if he doesn't leave then you are going to call the police, so I did. When I said that it only escalated to the point he was hitting his vehicle with his fist, I immediately ran inside, locked the doors, and went to bed. Eventually I heard his vehicle start up and Edward left. I was so relieved and so was Tammy Ann. I never expected to hear from again.

The next day at the grill, I for sure didn't think I would even see him so I wasn't really worried, but I also knew in my head that I had feelings for this man, I could not explain them but I did. I thought about him all day long and when I got off work and later that night, I called Edward. I asked him if we could talk and Edward replied talk. Edward then asked what we have to talk about. I suggested that we needed to talk about what had happened the previous night. Edward then said there was nothing to talk about and in his voice; I could tell he was drunk as usual. However, he did say he would come tomorrow and that we could talk. I said that would be fine. When I told my best friend Tammy Ann she told me I was crazy for even considering it, that he wasn't going to change and he didn't feel about me the way I did him. She said Michelle this man has been living with you for three months and what has he paid, while your working your butt off to make ends meet, having to borrow money from me to keep food on your table while Edward sits there and eats and does nothing to contribute in any way except by drinking. I couldn't say anything except hold my head down. But deep down I knew Tammy Ann was right but I still thought God had something to do with this relationship.

So once again we tried to make things work out but the whole time during this relationship never did I hear Edward apologize to me about anything. Christmas was approaching and I thought it would be a good idea so I made reservations to go to the mountains where we could spend some alone time together and I also thought Edward would like that. Edward never really traveled very much in his lifetime except going to the beach. But as for renting a cabin in the mountains, Edward had never been able to do that. He had also never had a real Christmas. Edward never ever had anything really nice in his life. He wore clothes that were from Wal-Mart and did not own any brand name clothes. There is nothing wrong with any of that, however, he just didn't want to spend the extra money, when it might be better spent in a bottle.

Edward is an electrician and so it wasn't like he didn't make any money but Edward spent his money on booze or on drugs. He did not spend his money on what was really important. That year was going to be our first Christmas together and I was bound and determined that we would have a wonderful holiday together. I made arrangements to take Edward on a three day vacation to the mountains. The lodge had a hot tub and I thought we both might enjoy that. I also bought him some new clothes that would replace all of his clothes in his closet. All of the shirts Edward owned had stains or holes in them; I even bought him some very expensive electrician boots and a very expensive electrician coat to keep him to warm while he was working outside.

Edward had never experienced a Christmas like that. Even my children gave him presents but he gave them nothing in return and it hurt their feelings something awful. So, I tried to replace what he didn't do with things from my own pocket book and would say they were from Edward but they knew better. Edward was always in the frame of mind that he had no children and he would not support anyone else's children in any kind of way. But it was Christmas and I thought he should have done at least one thing for them. However I kept reminding myself that he never had children so he didn't know how such those little things can make a huge difference in a child's life. When I spoke to Edward, about these things, he would ignore me or we would end up in an argument. So, I learned very quickly not to mention my children to him or mention Edward to my children. The thing was Edward didn't understand is that all children take advantage of their parents, they push parent's buttons, and they try to get away with anything they can and especially if they are teenagers. I agreed not to even mention my children to Edward because it seemed as if Edward did things with tough love however I do not agree with the ugly words such as cursing or belittling them when he wanted to say something to them, however not doing anything for them. So I thought Edward had no right to say anything to my children at all in any kind of way especially when they are almost grown and they have never had a man to do that to them before. All my children had ever had was me and I had been the Mother and the Father. What he didn't realize was that my children saw him taking advantage of me, eating from the grill for free, going on vacations, and Momma spending money on him when Edward never spent a dime on me. They tried really hard at the beginning to like him but he never once tried to give them a chance. Justin, Jordan and Meghan have the best hearts, I know my children and how much love and what they have to offer, and they tried with Edward. But they never got close to Edward at all. However, it was his fault entirely, not theirs because he was grown and they were not. I was a very protective Mother but when my children were wrong I always admitted they were wrong and made them go back and make things right by giving an apology.

Chapter 4 Learning more about Edward

At the time Edward came into my life my oldest son was in Afghanistan, so Justin never got to meet Edward until he arrived back home in October 2009. But Jordan and Meghan were there and for some reason Edward never saw anything good in either of children. Especially, Jordan and I could not understand why. Yes, Jordan was a handful, he tried me, he attempted things he knew he should not have been doing, but that was during the time he needed me the most. I also told myself I would never turn my back on any of my children no matter what the circumstances were. My parents had done that to me and I refused to do that to my children. I felt as if my parents had thrown me into a shark tank and I told me to either sink or swim.

I had such bad memories of how I had to sleep with men just to eat or to have a roof over my head. When my parents took Angel, they took part of me that I could never get back. And because of that, it made me become distant to everyone and caused me to have trust issues with everyone. I was always afraid to tell my past to anyone except Tammy Ann because I was afraid that people would judge me. I for sure did not want to tell Edward about my past. The whole little community we lived in believed that Edward was perfect. I even thought he was perfect. Too perfect actually, so I tried with all my might to show him how much I loved him. I didn't plan on falling in love with him but I did, then the needs of my children sort of took the back burner because of how Edward felt about them.

The night before Christmas which was Christmas Eve Edward and I had all our clothes packed up and went to bed early for our trip to go to the mountains. Right about midnight, Edward's cell phone rang and neither of us had any ideas about who might be calling so late. While I was lying next to him, I was able to listen to the entire conversation he had. When he answered the phone and said hello, I was shocked to hear a female voice come back to him. Edward acted like he had gotten caught. Just like a deer in head lights. I could hear every thing because it was so quite in my home. While they were talking, I over heard this girl ask him if she could come over to his house that night and he told her no not that night. Then she asked him if he was alone and he said yes even though I was lying right next to him. This hurt me so badly. When he finally got off the phone with the girl, that I later found out was a married woman, I asked him why he would lie to her as well as me? Why would he be having a relationship with a married woman much less tell her that he was alone and not even being at his house but being at mine. Edward said he did not know who it was, and then he said he did not know if it was his Mother or my daughter. I said Edward first off your Mother would never call you at midnight and second off my daughter would have never called your phone she would have called mine.

Edward thought I was an idiot. I was so disappointed, very upset, felt betrayed and again felt used and once again that is how my life has always have been. Needless to say, I knew Edward had lied to me and he knew I knew he lied, but I did not feel like arguing more about the situation.

So as Edward and I left the next day to go to the mountains for his Christmas present. I had asked my Mother if she would help run the grill while I was gone. I knew she would because when it comes to ordering people around she surely can do that. Momma was a dry person, a sad person, and a person that had the personality of a statue.

While I was gone for a few days and without my knowledge, my mother asked my sister Debbie to also come and help at the grill. I did not want Debbie there at all and my mother knew that. My children ate at the grill everyday. I didn't buy groceries for our home because we always had food at the grill and they knew what was available and knew that I allowed them to come in and eat whatever they wanted. I had also given them permission that if they needed money they could get it from the cash register at the grill. The very most they would take was usually around twenty dollars.

So the day of arriving to the mountains with Edward which we drove my car because the two vehicles he had was not dependable enough to go that distance which was about a six hour drive and of coarse I didn't feel safe in either of his vehicle's. So any time we went anywhere as a couple we always had to drive my car, and that sort of bothered me as well because anywhere we went not only did I have to drive but I also had to pay for the gas as well, but as usual I didn't think I deserved any better. As we arrived to the cabin we looked inside and all I could say is wow, I really needed this little vacation also because of being so tired from all the hard work and long days from the grill and from working so many hours at the grill for two years. This was the very first vacation I had for over five years and it was well deserved.

We started unpacking our clothes and immediately my cell phone started ringing, there was trouble at the grill. My Mother, my sister Debbie and my children Justin, Jordan and Meghan were having a huge disagreement. While I was receiving phone calls from both my Mother, sister I was also receiving phone calls from my children. I tried really hard not to take sides, which made my Mother and sister mad, and it hurt my children, but all I was trying to do is keep the peace. In my children's eyes, the grill belonged to them as much as it did to me, and I felt the same way because they worked just as hard at the grill as I did. But, in my Mother and my sister's opinion, they felt as if they were the owners while I wasn't there. So, they wouldn't allow my children to eat at the grill and that was what my kids were accustomed to.

So, this escalated and it got badly very quickly, to the point that the police were called to my grill twice in one day and my children were told to go home. My children had no food at home, nor did they have any money because of not being able to get money from the grill, as they were use to. It got so bad that my brother Joe and brother in law Kyle were chasing my children around the parking lot. Then they started man handling my kids. My kids were punched, scratched, and bitten. There were bruises, bite marks, and blood to prove it.

I couldn't believe this. I had more business on the outside of the grill than actual business inside of the grill. So, while all of this was happening, my friend Tammy Ann stepped in and took care of my children. She fed them and gave them some money until I returned. Everyone in the small community where we live have police scanners and they were all so curious as to what was happening down at the grill that when they heard all the commotion that was going on at my grill they came out to gawk. The crowd got so large, watching my family run my kids off, that there were actually people blocking traffic just to see what was going on.

Can you just imagine? I'm on vacation six hours a way from my children, and my children are running from their Uncle's outside of the grill because their Grandmother and Aunt wouldn't even allow them to eat. By this time I was furious, I didn't even know what to say to either party. I was so sad, mad, and hurt because once again, my family had hurt me. But this time it wasn't just me they had hurt but my children as well. I was afraid that this time my family might even cost me my business.

I pretended to have a good time at the cabin but I also was in a hurry to get home to see what was going on. But it is hard to have a good time when the person that you are with stays drunk the whole time. Edward did not even want to leave the cabin to go to dinner. I ended up paying for the whole trip and not only that but that was the weekend Edward introduced me to cocaine for the very first time. My parents claimed, years before that I was on cocaine and that is how they got custody of Angel but I had not even tried it at that point. I did not like the feeling it gave me at all, it just made me nervous and I couldn't sleep, I knew this wasn't me. I also was drinking and that also was something I never did that much in my life either.

I had so many terrible things running in my head, I didn't know what to do or how to even fix the problem at home or at the grill. As we were packing to go home, the whole time I was thinking, why does this stuff keep happening? Why can't I find someone to love me as much as I love them? Why can't people love hard the way I love hard? I was totally disappointed with this vacation and at the same time all that was running in my head, my thoughts made me think that I was the common denominator in all of the things that were bad in my life. That made me sad as well, because I thought something was very wrong with me.

Thinking of these things brought me back to a time in my life that my Mother had taken me to this place in Goldsboro, NC that was for bad children, or should I say bad teenagers. I remember when she drove me out there; she had been prepared for them to keep me there. She had even packed my clothes because she just knew they would keep me in this facility. After being interviewed by the gentleman in charge, he spent, what seemed like forever asking me question after question until finally he said that we were done. I was scared of what he was going to tell my Mother. When this gentleman got out of his chair to call my Mother in the room, I remember my hands being so sweaty feeling, and I my face was feeling so flushed and I was feeling so hot as if I was going to pass out.

The gentleman started telling my Mother that there was NOTHING wrong with me. The look on her face was priceless and filled with total disappointment. She sat there and argued with this man, whom I later found out, was a mental therapist that worked in this mental hospital for teenagers. Finally remembering back I had someone that was on my side, but as usual my Mother was trying to do what ever she could do to belittle me once again. Again, the doctors told my mom that there wasn't anything wrong with me and she would just get angry. If just one person would have asked me why I was acting out, I would have told them. However not once, even the Dr. she took me to see ever asked me what was going on. The problem was not me it was my Mother.

So, as I was packing our clothes from the mountains to return home, I couldn't pack quick enough. The whole ride home my head was racing with childhood thoughts of my Mother. I thought that if she could do some of the things she had done to me, what she was capable of doing to my children. Plus I was afraid of what my sister Debbie might do to my children as well.

So returning home I had to go to my parents home to pick up the money and receipts from the grill. When we arrived my Father sat there and didn't even say one word to me at the beginning but when he finally spoke up it was only to tell me how he had no use for my children and that he thought they were not worth shit. While he was saying these things about my children, I kept quite in order to show my father some respect but I did look over at Edward to see what his reaction was to what my father was saying. Edward seemed to be taking it all in and while my father was saying these horrible things he had this smirk grin on his face. Well, that just made me even angrier than I already was at my parents. Meanwhile, my Mother was cold as ice as well and just looked at me with these evil eyes as she had done so often when I was a child. I didn't know what to do or say. I was so uncomfortable that all I wanted to do was to get my money, my receipts, and leave so that is what I did.

After leaving their home I was talking to Edward, about all of this and I was shocked because he actually took my parents side. That did not sit well with me at all, because Edward knew nothing about how they had treated me in the past nor my children's past. He didn't know or understand how they never helped us when we needed them. My parent's never admitted how they treated me and how they have treated my children. None of my children's pictures were ever on my parent's walls or any of my pictures however, everyone else in my family such as all my siblings, their children even in-laws were up but not us. That sure did make you feel very welcome to go to their home.

When we finally reached my home, I saw the bite marks on my son Justin's arm done by my sister Debbie and the bruises. I told them that I was so very sorry and apologized for leaving them. It was so terrible and I felt as if I had let my own children down. When I talked to my children about all the chaos that had taken place while I was gone I promised them I would never do that again, and leave my Mother in charge ever again and I also promised them I would never do to them children as my parent's have done to me. I felt like a liar to my children because I promised them years ago I would never let them down like my parent's have let me down during my life as a child and as an adult but when I took this trip I felt as I did let them down. I felt as if I made my children feel the same hurt I felt when I was a child. I did not like that at all. I couldn't apologize enough.

As business kept getting worse and worse, the old feelings were coming back once again; I didn't know what to do, or whom to turn to. My parents and I barely spoke anymore and lost any ground we had gained in our relationship after the incident. I was losing everything once again. I again blamed myself for everything I had lost again, and had to sell the grill because my business had gotten so bad after all the chaos my Mother and my sister Debbie did while I was gone to the mountains with Edward. I had no money, just enough to pay my bills and barely able to cover that.

I had a nervous breakdown, and all day for several months I wouldn't even leave my house. I was so depressed and when Edward would come home I would hide it, I was not honest with him, again I was trying to live this pretend life, so I began telling him lies telling him I had way more than I actually had. Because he was all about money and that seemed to be his only love in life. Never ever, did I tell him how many times I've been married, how many times that I've been in trouble?

How in the world do you tell someone you lost your first daughter? I knew telling him all these things that have happened to me would make him run, so I lied. I never thought I would be good enough for Edward much less feeling good about me. I didn't like me, for years when I looked in the mirror I hated myself, I have blamed myself forever, hated myself forever, and forever thinking I was the very worse Mom ever. Always remembering how I could never let go of what had happened to Angel, this event affected every aspect of my life, and besides Edward and our relationship that wasn't ever going to be serious any way's, so it didn't bother me to lie to him.

It came a day Jordan was in serious trouble and he was getting ready to go to jail for driving without a license because he had several tickets without having a seat belt on. They took his license but he continued driving. Well they had a warrant for arrest and in order to get this issue resolved I had to come up with twenty-two hundred dollars. I had promised myself many years before that my children would never have to go through the same types of things that I had gone through. So, in order to come up with the money, I forced myself to sleep with a logger and he gave me the money I needed to help Jordan. That hurt me so badly. I felt so dirty because I had not done anything like that since I had lived in a barn, many, many years before. When I told Jordan what I had to do, he cried and said that he was so very sorry and after that day, my son has not been in trouble since.

I continued seeing Edward and little by little the threads were unraveling. He began to ask my children questions about the relationship that I had with the girl I use to live with. But he did not ask me any of those questions. Jordan over heard the conversation Edward was having with Meghan and Jordan went in the kitchen where they were and told Edward that if he wanted to know about me then he could ask me, not my kids. I was grateful for that, Jordan stood up for me.

When Justin wasn't home, Jordan took his place and became the man of the house. My children were very protective of me, and loved me dearly, no matter how my family that consisted of my parents and my siblings and niece and nephew's felt about me. While they grew up my children were barely around any of them, and when we had to move back here because of my sickness of having MS my children cried and cried. They didn't like it here at all in this small town. My children also never liked my family either. If there was an event that we were invited to, that pertained to my Mother's birthday my children never wanted to go. But usually they would go for me because they knew how I felt about the situation and how desperately I wanted to be a part of my family. My children knew they would never change however I still held on to faith, and just knew God would work all this out. But, my children didn't consider them as our family. They always said our family was in Georgia, and they were right.

My boys Justin and Jordan called Meghan's grandparents their grandparents, and Meghan's Dad was to them their Dad as well. Meghan's grandparents still to this day have my picture and my children's pictures on their walls her grandparents still treat me like their daughter. Even though my boys were no blood relations to them, they still considered them family. This too, was something Edward never understood. When Meghan's dad would come and visit, it would upset Edward tremendously. If it wasn't about money Edward couldn't understand it. He did not understand what it meant to have a loving family nor did he understand how to be a part of a loving family.

One particular time Meghan's Dad, his new wife, and two step sons came for a visit at my home. Meghan's Dad decided he wanted to grill out, but I didn't have a grill so Edward offered to let him borrow his grill. So, the guys went and loaded up his grill. While they were gone, they were going to stop at the grocery store to pick up everything we would need to eat. When they did this, I just knew Edward would offer to pay for our steaks, but to my surprise, he didn't. That made me feel embarrassed and before Meghan's dad left, I gave him money for half the bill at the grocery store.

More and more I was realizing just how tight Edward was with his money and how much Edward was just about himself. When Meghan's dad left, I did ask Edward why he didn't help Meghan's dad pay for at least half the groceries. The comment I got from Edward was so painful and this remark told me a lot about him, he said, "I do not have children and will not pay or support someone else's children." That comment really hurt my feelings and told me exactly how he felt about me and my children. This really created a huge argument, and that night he left and I might add he was drunk as usual and he went home. I thought to myself how can a man get into a vehicle drunk and possibly killing himself or someone else.

When he got home, I knew he was safe because he was blowing up my phone by calling and calling, I never answered. I called Tammy Ann and then that's when I told her everything, which she already knew what was going on, she just didn't say anything because she loved me and she knew how I felt about Edward. Tammy Ann told me to let him stay in his piece of crap house and never look back, but I told her maybe if I come clean with Edward then maybe things would change, she said "Michelle are you crazy?" Then Tammy Ann said, "Michelle look at what he has done to you." Then she went on to describe exactly what he had done for me during the entire time of our relationship. Which was absolutely zero? She also reminded me that he had done a back ground check on me and that he had also called someone we went to school with to find more information out about you. Then she asked why is it so important to him to know everything about you when you still know nothing about him, nor does he do anything for you there at your home but use you. Then she told me to count my losses and move on. I then told her I felt like I do not deserve any better, and maybe he would change if he knew everything. Tammy Ann was furious with me, and just couldn't understand why I wanted him so badly much less love him; however in my head I just knew I didn't deserve any one better.

Chapter 5 Coming Clean with Edward

I finally came clean with Edward about most everything, I only came clean about the money but nothing else, because I knew he would judge me as everyone else has done to me all during my life. I did tell him about the girl that I lived with and the lines got crossed but nothing more; I finally had to get a part time job just to try to keep the bills up. So I got a job working at a lawn mower shop repairing lawn mowers, the heat was so bad for my MS and when I would come home at night I would cry from the pain, I felt in my legs. But, I still wouldn't ask Edward for anything even though he was there every night. The reasons I did not ask him for anything was because of how he had treated Meghan's Dad and the things he had said then and how it hurt my feelings so much. Edward never paid one bill in my house and he lived with me for fourteen months.

Once in a while Edward would buy a few groceries on weekends to grill out for us. One night about midnight his cell phone started ringing, and he and I had been together now for many months. When he answered, I heard the same girl ask him if he was alone and he said "yes" even though I was laying right there beside him. After he hung up, I asked him about it and asked him why he lied about it. He gave me the same lame answer he had given me before about he wasn't sure who it was on the phone; at that moment, I knew that was bull. That was the same married woman he claimed to be just friends with. However, I have been around the block way more than him and I wasn't stupid. So I asked why a married woman would call you at midnight, and of coarse he had more excuses. If anyone in this world can spot a lie it is someone that has lied a lot themselves which would include me. I have lied and have been lied to all my life and when it came to lying, I was taught very well. I immediately knew he was lying, and again I never got an apology from him never.

All that did was create more and more insecurities within me, and when I tried to talk to Edward about my insecurities he played it off as if it was all in my head. Just as my family had done to me, years before he tried to convince me I was crazy. The few nights that he didn't stay with me, I always thought it was because he was with someone else, he never took me to his home, and I had never seen the inside of his home after being together for fourteen months, but I would go there and mow the yard and weed eat the ditches. I never even got a thank you when I did this. Again, this would make Tammy Ann furious with me. When I sold the grill, I spent it all on him, as we were getting more serious I thought. So then, I thought maybe it would be a good idea that we took another vacation and this time I wanted to go on a cruise to get far as I could away from this small town.

As usual I paid for that as well, Edward would spend money on this cruise but only for beer or mixed drinks and for the casino, and Edward again stayed drunk as he did when I took him to the mountains and during the cruise I always found Edward in the casino playing blackjack. Edward thought he was actually good at blackjack but he would always take cards he shouldn't of and lost hundreds and hundreds of dollars and I seen this and wondered why he couldn't do anything for me at home. I never ever asked Edward about his financial situation, however I knew he was saving a bunch of money because I paid all the bills at my house and he was there for over fourteen months and paid nothing. He seen me struggle and he knew I had MS and working in the heat doing a man's job at the lawn mower shop which was very bad for my MS. It didn't seem to matter to Edward that I was working in a lawn mower shop like a man, just as long as I didn't ask Edward for any money. I came home and I could barely walk. I smelt like burnt oil and I was so tired.

So, while we were on the ship I was thinking about all of this, watching him spend money like crazy, and after paying for the complete cruise by myself I had no money. So I couldn't even bring home any souvenirs for my children, or for my best friend Tammy Ann, and on top of it I was having a miserable time once again, and only wanting to go home. I couldn't wait to get off that ship and return home to my children. I once again felt like all I was is a woman that was nothing but a person that only wanted to please, even if the other person didn't want to please me any at all. The whole time on that ship Edward spent over nine hundred dollars on alcohol not to mention what he lost in that casino. Edward didn't get me anything nor did he ever offer to get me anything. While we were on the cruise all I kept thinking about was I was nothing but a whore to Edward, he didn't show me any love and he never told me he loved me.

I had learned a long time ago words are just words but actions speak the loudest and he sure didn't show me any actions towards me when it came to loving me or my children. When returning home from this cruise he and I talked and I told him I would not continue on living with him, I had been patient enough and had been through enough without some kind of commitment from him. I was very serious and he didn't like what I had to say. So, the ride home, which was a two hour drive home, was also a very miserable ride home.

So as I was riding home I knew what I was going to do when I reached home, and that was to pack all his stuff up, all his clothes I had bought him, all his belongings and he would be leaving my home and I told him this while we were driving home. While telling him this all Edward had on his face was a blank look, he didn't say anything, but I could tell on his face that he did not like what I was saying because his gravy train ride was coming to an end. For fourteen months each week he was able to pocket every single check he had made. Later I found out, that he was bringing home about seven hundred dollars a week. I figured it out to be that he had saved almost thirty two thousand dollars by living with me, because he didn't pay one bill at my home, he didn't have to pay gas to go to his work because his company supplied him with a work van and they supplied the gas as well. The more I thought about all of this the angrier I became. Edward had done nothing but take advantage of me knowing I had children to support, and a home that had bills, and he didn't offer to help me in any way.

So, as we were still driving home and as I was figuring out the money, he was saving I brought it to his attention. When I did that he became even angrier, and then he called me a gold digger. I laughed and said, "No, you are the gold digger. You are a man that cares nothing about anything but your beer; your weed that you smoke, your cigarettes and you are all about yourself." After that, not one word was spoken the rest of the way to my house.

When I walked in the house, I hugged Jordan and Meghan and they knew something was wrong by the look on my face. They watched while I collected garbage bags and went to my bedroom. My children stood at the bedroom door, watched while I gathered all of Edward's things up, and stuffed it in garbage bags. As I was filling bag after bag I was taking them and loading them in his truck. I had this look on my face that reminded me of the look my Mother would give to me while I was a child, all I wanted was for him to leave and never look back.

I felt used, I felt as if he didn't love me like he claimed. He for sure didn't care about my children. I had already had made it very clear to him that I believed that God had not made more perfect kids than my own. Then all of a sudden he said the word "Jam." I asked him what did that mean. I thought he was talking about jelly or something but no, he was talking about my second son Jordan. His full name was Jordan Allen Molsen, which made his initials JAM. So, I asked him what did mean by that and he said out loud so my children could hear it, "JAM means "Just Another Mistake." OMG, when he said that it was like a slap in my face and I was furious. I couldn't pack his bags quick enough, I was crying so hard, after I had done so much for this man I couldn't believe he would say such terrible things about my children that he wouldn't even give a chance too.

His heart reminded me so much as my Mother's, his heart was as cold as her heart. Edward also loved money just like she did; it seemed to me that he was all about monetary things the same as my Mother. He seemed to be happy as long as I was doing everything in my home, paying for all the bills, buying and cooking all the meals, cleaning everything that needed to be cleaned in my home, washing and drying all the clothes, not mentioning folding all the clothes and putting them up. I was also working a full time job by this time in a lawn mower shop, which was really bad for my MS.

Why would Edward want to leave? Edward had it made, he was saving every cent he was making, and I was struggling and dirt poor from trying to keep up with the bills and taking care of my home responsibilities. Not to mention every time I mowed my yard, I mowed his as well. Then he had the audacity to talk negatively about my children.

At this point, I have had enough. Finally, he was gone and he stayed gone for a couple of weeks, and then I received a phone call from Edward. Again, it was a late call, and of coarse he was drunk, I could tell by the way he was talking. I asked Edward what he wanted and he told me he missed me. Deep down I missed him also but I didn't miss his behavior or his drinking. At that time, he didn't know that I had quit working at the lawn mower shop due to my MS. My MS had flared up terribly from being so upset over Edward and the heat from working outside at the lawn mower shop. It got so bad that I was forced to use a walker. Tammy Ann was helping me out by going to pay some bills for me and also going to the grocery store, getting groceries while Jordan was at work, and Meghan was at school. Tammy Ann also brought me lunch while the children were gone during the day.

When Edward called I didn't tell him any of this, I didn't want him to know that my MS had flared up because of him. I also did not want him to think that I needed him in any way. I didn't want to give Edward any kind of satisfaction what so ever that he had maybe done this to me. But I did miss Edward and I have to admit it felt really good to hear his voice even though he was drunk. It made me think maybe by me kicking him out made him do some thinking. But, during the entire conversation Edward never apologized for the things he said about my children, nor did he apologize to me for his actions of how he never contributed to anything that had to be done to help me run my home properly.

Once again, I tried to explain to him that he couldn't just live with me for fourteen months and not contribute anything while I was struggling to do everything. It was extremely hard for me to keep things a float. I was only living on disability at the time and my house payment was five hundred dollars a month. Just the house payment alone took half my check and I told him this. Edward remained silent once again. So, when he stopped talking so did I. Finally I heard Edward say HELLO and I said HELLO back. After that Edward asked, "Michelle what do you want me to do, pay your bills?" I said, "No but that he should help out with the bills if he was going to live with me again like he had before."

I should have known how Edward would feel and respond. It turned into another argument, and then Edward hung the phone up on me. Immediately after he hung up on me I called Tammy Ann, and I was crying and was totally upset. I even told her I didn't care if I lived or died. She told me he was not worth that and all he was doing was playing games and trying to mess with my head as if I had done wrong instead of him. However all my life I felt I was always the one that was wrong, not ever having any confidence in myself wha

I was feeling so depressed about not being able to walk, and struggling with everything in my life financially and emotionally. I didn't have any kind of support from my family after the grill closed. My family made me feels as if I was a total loser. After the grill closed my family never called me again, nor did they ever come and see me at my home, things were right back where it had been before the grill. I was so confused, I couldn't understand, and felt so unloved by everyone. Before Edward hung up on me, I even told him the same things that I told Tammy Ann about how I was feeling unloved.

About an hour, later Edward was at my house. He had called my sister Debbie and told her that he thought I was going crazy. So, Debbie, Edward, and the police showed up at my house in order to take me and put me in the mental ward at the local hospital. When I finally realized what was going on I immediately called Tammy Ann. She dropped everything she was doing and came over to my house. Thankfully, the policeman that came to my home was related to Tammy Ann. She was able to explain the situation to her nephew and told him that all I wanted was for Edward to leave.

All of a sudden, Edward told the officer that I had taken a bunch of pills. The officer looked at me and asked me if that was true and of course, I said NO! Tammy Ann also vouched for me and told the officer as well that wasn't true. So, then the officer asked Edward whether or not this was his home, and he replied no. The officer then told him to leave and that is what he did. But, when Edward left, he gave me a look that I have never seen from him before. Edward was extremely angry.

Tammy Ann and I were angry as well. I could not believe or understand why Edward had called my sister, Debbie. I also could not understand why they had called the police on me. Everything had been based on a lie from him and my sister Debbie had gone along with it. Of course, my sister Debbie hated me but she knew next to nothing about my relationship with Edward. She didn't know that Edward had sponged off me for over fourteen months.

At this time Tammy Ann was starting to realize everything I had told her about my family was sad but true. After all the chaos, she sat down with me because I was already sick with my MS and told me to stay away from them all including Edward and my family. She knew how I felt about him, but she told me the reason I felt that way was because I didn't feel the way I should about myself. Tammy Ann was right and I told her she was right but I just didn't know how to escape all the feelings I was feeling and have felt all my life.

I told her this is how I have felt since I was just twelve years of age. The very day when I heard my own Mother say to someone on the phone about how it was my fault the reason she lost her first daughter Carrie. Tammy Ann tried her best getting me out of that house trying to make me feel better about myself, she truly loved me as her best friend, and I knew that. Even her own family loved me, her children Casey and Christine, and her husband Brent and even her Mother and Father accepted me as one of their own, and even accepted my children. I loved living next door to her and she loved me living next door to her. We were a whole lot alike, we were both clean freaks, and loved to have clean vehicles, and a clean yard, and we both worked our tails off to keep things on that little corner looking just that way. Tammy Ann and Brent had this amazing marriage, a marriage I wanted so badly like hers.

Chapter 6 Coming back Together so I Thought

One afternoon Tammy Ann and I were on the swing outside and we were just talking. I had asked Tammy Ann if she and Brent had ever had problems like Edward and I had. She gave me a look and I realized that she knew that I was thinking about going back to Edward and trying hard to work things out with him. Tammy Ann admitted that she and her husband had some problems but they had never been to the extent that Edward and I had gone through.

She said Brent had always been a provider and a person that always took care of his family. I shook my head yes but I said to Tammy Ann I can see that but would he still be like that if your and his children were just yours? Immediately she said yes and told me how and why, she said Brent's dad wasn't really his own dad but to Brent he was, he was a way better dad than the dad he actually had. While we were discussing everything, she had told me that I deserved someone better. I deserved to have a husband like hers and I knew she was right.

While she was telling me about Brent and all he did for his family, I realized that I had never seen or heard of a marriage like that. To me she was describing a Cinderella story that was only in fairy tale story books. I had several failed marriages feeling like Elizabeth Taylor and not one of them ever treated me the way she was saying Brent treated her. I told her that I was considering calling Edward back, I could tell by her reactions she did not like that idea whatsoever, and wondered why I would even want to do that. Tammy Ann just sat there looking at the ground while I was crying, and I told her that I loved him.

She then said Michelle how can you love him. What has he done for you except hurt you ever since you met him? Then she asked me if Edward had ever even taken me out on a real date. Has Edward ever paid one bill for you? Did Edward even care about your health when you were working at that lawn mower shop? Does Edward even care about your MS problems? Then she reminded me how Edward and my sister Debbie wanted to put me in the mental ward at the local hospital, and reminded me if it wasn't for her they would have probably succeeded. I just looked at her with this blank face not knowing what to say, and then all of a sudden she said what about the back ground check Edward did?

Tammy Ann then asked me, "Michelle do you know anymore about Edward today then you did fourteen months ago." I couldn't speak because I knew everything she was saying was true. Then Tammy Ann said to me Michelle I know everything about you, and have I once ever judged you? I said NO. Then she said what little Edward did know about you how many times has he thrown this in your face, I replied a lot. When I said that Tammy Ann said this should be enough to not want him back in your life, do you want to keep going through all this day in and day out? I said No.

Then I looked at her and said well maybe he would change. Maybe he does not know how to love, maybe I can teach him. While I was talking, she did nothing but shake her head in a negative way. But, when she saw my face, she that she could not persuade me to find a different man so she told me that she loved me but that she couldn't make my decisions for me. She explained that she just did not want to see me treated badly any more by Edward. After that comment, she then said to me Michelle you have been through enough between your family and with your children acting up at times, and with the grill you had to sell, and then with all the drama with Edward. She looked at me and then said Michelle all I want for you is the very best, and in my opinion Edward just is not that person, but I cannot tell you what to do, you have to do what your heart tells you to do.

Then she said, "Girl, I love you like my sister." When she said that I looked at her and we just hugged and cried together. Tammy Ann was a true friend. She was the only one that been there for me while everything in my life was coming unraveled. Tammy Ann reminded me that not even my parents had been there for me when I needed them. Then she asked, "Michelle have they even called you to see how you were doing?" I told her that I was so used to their behavior.

We then talked about how my family had gone years at a time, never including me or my children in any holiday events, or even any family dinners. I told her I have learned from the times in my life, that they only come in my life when things are going good, so they can get whatever I could give them. But when times are hard and they know that, they never come around. I told her that they do not love me, nor have I ever had parents that cared about my interest. I then told her, Tammy Ann you have known me now six years and I have been in the hospital several times, and while you were there spending the nights with me, did my family ever come to even visit me?

After that remark, I said you know what hurts me the most is my brother Joe is a pastor and he would help others that did drugs and had alcohol problems but he would never come and see his sister. I told her it hurts, especially when I have tried so hard to get their approval, but to me it seems as if they are very ashamed of me. I said then Tammy Ann do you know how much it hurts.

I then looked at her and I said I am going to tell you something I have never shared with anyone, she then turned her head towards me and looked at me right into my eyes, as I was crying I told her something that Angel told me a very long time ago. Angel said while she was growing up and when people would ask my parents how many children they had, my parents would only say three, meaning Joe, Debbie, and Angel. I looked at Tammy Ann and said now do you understand how I am just broken down? I said to Tammy Ann how would you feel if you walked into your parent's home and didn't see your pictures of you and your family but seen only pictures of your siblings and their spouses and their children? Just how would you feel? She said nothing, she just couldn't understand. I then looked at her and said Tammy Ann my parents completely left Carrie and myself out in the cold and acted as if we and our children were never a part of their family along with our children. Then I told her by my own parents doing that it made me feel like if as I wasn't part of the family but when I had the grill, they couldn't get enough, they saw me all the time and now that I do not have the grill, I do not have them.

I told Tammy Ann I have gone most of my life without any family, other than my children. She then told me that I did have a family. I had her family. I knew she meant well and I really appreciated that but I still had a hole in my heart from my own family. I wanted my family, and needed them so much, but they were never there for me, or did they ever care to hear my problems. If I did talk to them, the conversations were so cold feeling. It was as if they really didn't care what was going on in my life, nor did they really want to hear what I had to say or what was going on in my life.

Each time I went to my parents' house, I would end up crying all the way home because of their hatefulness. I never felt welcomed, and my children were not even allowed to even go to my parent's home. I just couldn't wrap my head around that. To me no matter what my children have done, I would never tell my children they could not come to my home. As I was telling Tammy Ann all of this, she asked me if that is what is happening why you continue putting yourself through that. I replied back to her the same thing I told my children. I looked at her with tears flowing down my face, and I could barely speak and said because I love them. Tammy Ann along with my children just couldn't understand after the way they have treated me. I just kept holding on to faith that things in my own family would get better and still to this day, I pray really hard for this reunion from God with my family.

After the conversation with Tammy Ann, I went back into the house and I was really depressed. I knew that depression ran in my family but I wondered if my mother's hateful genes ran over into me as well. My mother had received her hatefulness from her mother. My Grandmother was not a loving person. So, I know that my mother learned how to be un-loving from her mother. My Mother did to me what her mother had done to me when I was growing up. My Grandmother was a very confused, sad, emotionally disturbed person. She was somewhat mentally disturbed and I believe that is why my Mother had similar problems of not being able to connect emotionally with her own children.

I know that I don't have problems connecting with my children. I am a very protective Mother, and would do anything for my children. My children know and understand that if they need to talk they always call their Mother. My kids and I have always been able to talk about whatever was bothering them. For me if my children have a problem then I have a problem. If they need my help then I do whatever I can to help in any way possible. If it is just to talk, I talk to them or if they need advice, I do my best to give them advice, if they need help with money I do my best to help with that also and make payment arrangements so they can pay me back. My children are my life, because for many, many years and almost my whole life they were all I have ever had. When Justin was in Afghanistan, my parents never ever asked if I had heard from him, which really bothered me tremendously. My family acted towards my children, the same as Edward acted towards my children.

After talking to Tammy Ann, and I pulled myself together I called Edward and asked if we could talk. Edward then asked me what we needed to talk about. I replied back to Edward that I think we need to talk about our relationship; he got silent on the phone, as usual. I then said would you like to come over and eat dinner. Edward then replied that it would be late because he had things to do after work. I then asked how late? He said about eight or eight thirty. I didn't like it but I agreed. I was wondering what he had to do after work and what was preventing him that was going to keep him from coming over earlier than that.

Also, running in my head after I had made the phone call, I knew he was at work, and he really acted as if someone was with him and he didn't want that person to know about me, by the way he was talking. Again, I was feeling as if another person here on this earth was completely ashamed of me. When I would get those feelings, I would just pace back and forth in my house. I would also stand at the kitchen window and just look outside, to the point I would have hard knots in my elbows from leaning on the counter at the kitchen sink looking out the window.

As I was leaning on the counter, I was debating on what I would cook for dinner. It was cool outside so I decided to cook some homemade hamburger vegetable soup, knowing that could be enough for the next day. After I was getting the soup all into a big pot, I then went and took a shower. I wanted to look nice when Edward arrived but from the way he talked on the phone I was not sure he would even show up. I waited and waited, dinner was ready, I had taken my shower, and everything was already prepared.

My stomach was in knots, not knowing how I was going to talk to him about our relationship, and the things I expected from him in this relationship if it would be able to continue. I didn't know how Edward would take the news about how I was feeling, and if Edward was feeling the same as me. I was pacing and pacing, Meghan was at work, and Jordan was at one of his friend's home playing basketball. So I knew it would just be the two of us, I knew Edward would like that, because Edward didn't care for my children at all and seemed like Edward only liked it when it was just the two of us. Edward was a man that was forty two years of age, never been married, and never had any children of his own. In my mind I knew Edward was not the type to want to be married however I wasn't going to continue allowing a man to be here every night, living with me and sleeping in my bed without some kind of commitment, and that meant getting engaged, and eventually getting married.

Eventually he arrived, and when I went to the door, he looked so good; Edward was a very handsome man however I had always heard, "Pretty is what Pretty does." When he walked, into the living room, Edward and I hugged. And he smelled so good to me. When I hugged him it reminded me how my mother use to hug me and that was with a one arm hug, meaning he really did not want to hug me and then I noticed he had a bag with him and of coarse there was beer in the bag. Again, I didn't like that but I was so happy he was there. Before Edward would even eat his dinner, I had prepared for us, he immediately started drinking his beer, and then he asked me if I wanted one. I didn't like beer but I agreed to drink one, when I took a sip it would make my lips turn upside down.

When Edward saw my frown he laughed and said, drinking beer is an acquired taste. I didn't like it but to satisfy him I continued drinking the beer. After Edward drank enough beer, he finally wanted to eat his dinner. I think I drank about two beers and because of not being a drinker, I was feeling drunk, walking unstable and not thinking clearly. We then ate our dinner, and after dinner I cleaned the kitchen up, while I was cleaning the kitchen up, Edward went to the living room, sat down, and was watching TV. I was washing the dishes and Edward asked me to bring him another beer, so I did. When I was done, I went into the living room where Edward was and sat on the couch next to him. As soon as I sat down, he started kissing me, and wow what a kisser Edward was. After that, one thing led to another, and before I knew it, we were in my bed and we were making love. Again, I didn't get to tell him what I wanted to tell him. Because of that, once again I felt like nothing but a whore, and felt as if that was the only reason he came over to my house. Again, just to use me, eat free and to satisfy him by sleeping with me. I felt totally ashamed once again and I didn't sleep well that night. While he was lying next to me snoring, all I could think about was our messed up relationship. I wanted to know what his intentions were in regards to our relationship.

Chapter 7 Finally telling him my conditions

The next morning when the alarm clock went off for him to go to work, I was already awake. I was already up and in the kitchen. While he was in the shower, my children Jordan and Meghan came out of their rooms, the look on there faces made me regret my actions even more. They didn't like him at all. The reason they didn't like him was because of the way he had treated me and them. They knew Edward was only using me. My children didn't say a word but I knew what they were thinking by the look on their faces. That morning they didn't even eat breakfast at home. They told me they would pick up something at McDonald's. They didn't want to stick around long enough to even see him. I completely understood and gave them a hug and kiss and some money to eat, and they left before Edward came out of my bedroom.

At that moment, I realized that I wasn't setting a good example for my children. Finally, Edward came out dressed for work. I had made him a breakfast sandwich to take with him and he surprised me by saying thank you. He had never thanked me for anything before and then he gave me a quick kiss and hug and then left to head for work. As he was walking out the door, I said, "Edward, I love you." He looked at me and replied, "OK." I couldn't believe it. All of the good things I had been thinking about him maybe changing for the better just flew out the window with that one word. Again, he left me feeling horrible.

When I am upset or thinking about something, I clean. So, I spent most of the morning cleaning and thinking. I thought about why I had done what I had done the night before. Then I thought about my kids and how it affected them and then I thought about what I was going to do. I decided that I would no longer call Edward. If he wanted to talk to me he could call me, my mind was made up. But, that was easier said than done. Every time I turned around, I was looking at the telephone willing it to ring, wanting it to be him. I even tried calling my friend Tammy Ann just to make sure the phone was working properly. I knew that was a mistake as soon as she asked what had happened the night before. I couldn't lie to her and although she never said anything, bad to me about what I had done I knew she was disappointed in me like my children had been.

While I was talking to Tammy Ann, she asked me if I wanted to go out and eat lunch, just get out of the house. I wanted to, but I had to tell her I couldn't because I didn't have any money. Tammy Ann then said Michelle I didn't ask you if you had money for lunch. I asked you if you wanted to go out and eat some lunch in order to get you out of that house. I said that I just couldn't because I really didn't have the money to spend on a lunch out. Then she said, "Michelle, I do not care if you do not have any money, I invited you out, so get yourself together and take your shower and let's go out to eat." I finally agreed to let her buy me lunch.

Tammy Ann knew I was depressed and she wanted to get my mind off Edward. That was a hard task, but as usual, I would put on a happy face and pretend like I always had. I just couldn't figure out why he treated me the way he did when I had done so much for him. All I could do was talk about Edward. Tammy Ann heard the same thing over and over. I am sure it really got on her nerves, but she was such a great friend to me that she always listened. She knew how depressed I was, and not only that she also knew she was the only person I could talk too. When I got something on my mind, it was so hard to just let it go. So, I would talk about it over and over, and replay it in my mind over and over. I just couldn't understand why Edward didn't want to know what I wanted to talk about the night before. I also could not understand why he had not called me yet. Just thinking about it all day, talking about it all day, I was making myself totally sick. Tammy Ann was losing patience with me, went, and got me something for my head because it was hurting so badly, then she gave me something to help me sleep so my headache would go away.

Finally, I went to sleep and then the phone rang I was hoping so badly it was Edward and it was, I looked at the clock and saw that it was about two thirty in the afternoon. I said hello and he replied with a "hey." Edward then asked me what I was doing. I said I was lying down because I had a really bad headache. Then I asked him if he was going to come home that night when he got off work. He hesitated and then finally said, "NO." I asked why not, and he said he was tired, and he wanted to get some rest. In my head, I knew he was lying to me, but I didn't say anything nor did I give him any indication that I was even upset. However, I was very upset. Well, after that he didn't act like he wanted to talk any more because the phone just remained silent between the both of us. So, he said, "well bye and I will talk to you later." I replied, "OK have a good day and have a good night." Edward then said, "You do the same," and we hung up.

When I hung up all I could do was cry. My heart felt totally broken. I thought to myself: once again, he didn't want to know what I wanted to talk about and he didn't even ask me about it. I quickly realized that he had gotten what he wanted from me, he was satisfied, that was all he wanted to begin with, and didn't even care what I even wanted to talk about. I didn't even have the guts to call Tammy Ann to tell her that he had called.

To my surprise, she called me not too long after he called, and wanted to know if I was feeling any better. I said yes but she knew me well enough that she knew I was not telling her the truth. She then asked me if Edward had called and I got quiet for a second, immediately after that she asked, "What did he want?" Reluctantly, I told her. I knew what she would say. I was right she said, "If I were you Michelle. I would go to his house tonight. Tell him exactly what you wanted to tell him the night before, and get it over with so you can either be with him the way you want to be or move on with your life. You can leave knowing you did the very best you could do by Edward. Stop wasting your time on someone that doesn't feel the same about you."

So, that is what I decided to do. Tammy Ann also suggested something that I prayed would not be true. I had thought about it but I really didn't want to know if there was, another girl was at his house. If that was the real reason he didn't want to come home, I didn't know how I would take that news.

So, I knew Meghan had to go to work again that night, and as usual when Jordan got off work, he always wanted to hang out with his friends. But, before they did any of that, they always came home to eat dinner. As the children came in from school and work, Meghan would do her homework and Jordan would do his laundry. Meghan and Jordan left after they ate their dinner. I cleaned up the kitchen, and then proceeded to get ready to go to Edward's home without his knowledge. I was so nervous, as usual, I was always thinking the very worst, and in my mind I just knew Edward had another girl at his house. If that was true, I asked myself what I was going to do. As I was thinking about this all, I was getting more and more nervous about going. However, I just knew I had to finally get my answers or move on without Edward.

So, as I was driving to his home, my head was racing again with all sorts of thoughts. How I got there, I do not know because it was like I was in a daze driving towards his home because of thinking so much. When I was reached his driveway, I noticed there were no lights on inside his house. But, you couldn't see any vehicles in his driveway unless you completely pulled all the way up into his driveway because he always parked his vehicles in his back yard. As I was approaching the back yard, I was so relieved to see the only cars parked were his work van, and his two old trucks. So, I felt much better about that and was thinking more positively. I still wasn't sure how he was going to feel about what I had to tell him, or how he would respond to what I had to say.

As I was getting out of my car and walking towards his back door, the back porch light came on. So, I knew he was home. I didn't have to knock because as I started up the stairs to the deck, he opened the door. I could tell from the way he was acting that he had already had a few beers. When I made it onto the deck, he was standing at the door, and he asked me what I was doing there. It sort of hurt my feelings, but I stood my ground and told him I needed to talk to him. Edward backed up as if he was giving me room to come into his home, so I did.

The first thing I noticed was he wasn't much of a house cleaner. I realized this was the first time I had ever been in his house since we had started dating. Edward didn't even hug or kiss me when I walked in. That told me he was not happy to see me. He walked into the living room, sat down in his chair, and asked, "Well, what's so important that you need to talk about now, that couldn't wait for another day."

That also hurt my feelings and I guess I had a sour look on my face because he commented on that as well. Edward was right; I knew that he did not really care for me when he did not show me any affection at all. My first words to Edward were, "I love you," He returned the words, I love you too. Then I asked him if he wouldn't mind turning off the TV for a few minutes while we talked. He did as I asked but reluctantly.

I then proceeded to tell him how I felt about our relationship. I told him that I didn't like the way our relationship was going. I told him that I was not a whore and someone he could just use at his own convenience and for his own personal satisfaction. I then told him I wanted a real relationship. That included marriage and a home we would share together. I then said that it was not fair to me the way things were going. I also wanted an answer or at the very least, I wanted to know how he felt about what I was saying. When I was finished talking he looked at me and said he that he needed to go through four seasons with me. I had to ask what he meant by that. Edward replied, "you know: summer, spring, winter, and fall." I said, "Edward we have already gone through five seasons together and I am done going through seasons with you."

When I said that, he knew I was no longer playing around. I told him that if I didn't receive an answer that this would be the last day of our seasons together. Then he looked at me and said, "You sure know how to ruin things." I asked what he meant by that. Edward replied that a woman was not supposed to ask a man to marry her; it was supposed to be the other way around. I said, "Edward I am not asking. I just want to know when you are going to ask." He gave me a strange look and said that he didn't know. I grabbed my purse and said OK I see how things are now. Then I said, "All you want from this relationship is to have someone to live with that will pay all the bills, will feed you, and wash your clothes. Most importantly you want someone to have sex with whenever YOU want it without having to commit to anything." I made it clear to him that I did not have to beg for someone to be with me. I thought that when two people loved each other and told each other that they were loved then the logical next step was marriage. I guess that was all a lie to get me to do all of the things I have done for you.

Then I said if two people love, one another they are suppose to help each other, and then I asked him what he had ever helped me to do. He looked down at his feet while I was talking. I told him that he had lived with me for fourteen months and that he had not paid for any of the bills that the house had made. I recognized that he had occasionally bought groceries but was usually when he wanted something. I brought up the fact that we never once used one of his vehicles to go anywhere because they weren't dependable. I complained that he never even offered to help me pay for gas.

I reminded him that he had told me at the beginning of our relationship the reason he had never dated before was because he didn't have a reliable car. Then he started getting loud and very boisterous. I stopped him as soon as he started yelling. I assured him that I had done him a favor after all of these months. He wanted to know how I had helped him. I told him that he had saved a lot of money because he never had to pay for anything. Edward then lowered his own voice and said that I should be grateful to him because he had helped me out also. I asked him what he thought he had helped me with. Edward replied that he had installed my water heater when it had broken down. I laugh and said that he benefited from the water heater but that I had been the one to pay for the heater.

I had finally had enough. I told Edward that this conversation was going nowhere. I knew the next day was going to be his last day of his work week so I told him that he had until the end of the next day to make his decision about our relationship. If he decided that he didn't want to continue then he was to come by my house one more time and pick up his belongings and that he would no longer be welcome. Then I walked out the door and said good-bye. I went home, afraid I might have made a mistake, but I knew with all my heart that I was tired of paying all the bills by myself. I was also tired of Edward mooching off of me, while he was saving every check he was making. I felt as it wasn't fair but I also knew I loved him as well, and I did want a commitment from him.

Chapter 8 Getting my answers

Returning home, I felt much better after telling him my conditions and was relieved to have the burden off my shoulders. I immediately called Tammy Ann and told her what had taken place at Edward's. I told her that I had stood my ground and told him exactly what I had planned to say. Tammy Ann said she was very proud of me. When I went to bed that night, I prayed to God that Edward would make the right decision, and come to his senses. The following morning, I was feeling better about myself, and what I had done the night before. I waited patiently for a time I would know Tammy Ann was up to talk to her once again. While waiting I got all my choirs done, thinking the whole time Edward would call me soon.

It was approaching ten o'clock that morning so I knew Tammy Ann was up. I called and of coarse she answered the phone, and as usual, we started talking again about Edward. After we talked for a while Tammy Ann asked me what I would do if he did not adhere to the rules I had given him. I had not really put much thought into what I would do if he refused me. Deep down I just knew Edward loved me, he just did not know how to show it like Brent did for Tammy Ann I tried to explain that to her. Tammy Ann hesitated and then told me not to get my hopes up because if Edward really loved me he would never have treated me the way he had. She continued by reminding me that all he had ever done the whole time living while living with me was use me and that the entire relationship has been nothing but a roller coaster ride. She pointed out that one minute would be great and the next minute I would be in tears. Tammy Ann then stated that Edward had never cared about me the way I deserved.

Edward had never been there for me when I had need of him. She reminded me that I was even too scared to ask him for any money. I knew she was right about that one, because I was. All Edward thought and talked about was money. Tammy Ann got me thinking about things I did not want to even think about. She reminded me of the horrible things Edward had said about my kids. We agreed that if anyone had said those things about her kids she would have kicked them to the curb. I then said Tammy Ann maybe he will change, and then said Tammy Ann you got to remember he never had any children and maybe in time he will change. I then told her I know he had many step-fathers in his life and I told her I just knew he would want to be a better step-father to my children than what he had in his life. After that, Tammy Ann said I hope so for you, because I know just how much you love him. She then left so I could do some more work around my house. I said OK, I will call you later when and if Edward calls and I will let you know what he says. She said OK I love you and I then said I love you too Tammy Ann.

It was approaching lunch time and that was the usual time Edward would call me, if he were going to call me. I was waiting so patiently for his call, pacing back and forth, as I usually did from one room to another, it was getting past the time he would have called but he did not call. I was getting so sad, mad, and very emotionally torn, because I knew I had put everything I had into this relationship and he gave nothing in return. I had turned my head to so many bad things he had done to me this entire time while he had been living with me the whole fourteen months.

So, for the next few hours, I lay on the couch thinking about everything Tammy Ann and I had talked about. And, I went over in my head all the things Edward had done to me and how he had repeatedly used me. All of these depressing thoughts made my mind bring all of my demons to the front of my mind. Things like Angel, my mother, jail, and the fact that all four of my children had different fathers. It made me so depressed that I lay there in tears until my son Jordan came home from work. As soon as my son came in from work he knew I had been crying and asked me what was wrong. I told him what had happened and he said, "Momma, you're a great Mom, and you are a great person." He told me not to worry about Edward and that it was his loss. Then he then hugged me and rubbed my head because I had such a headache and told me loved me.

Jordan then said Momma "Edward is stupid." However, I knew Jordan didn't like Edward anymore than Edward liked Jordan. After that, he said, "Momma are you going to be alright while I go and hang out with my friends?" I told him I was going to be fine, and he asked me to stop crying, I told Jordan that it seemed like I had done nothing but mess my entire life up. He tried to convince me that I had not.

I got up from the couch because I knew I was hurting Jordan from talking about my past and talking about Edward. I knew he hated it when I would get depressed, so I stopped talking about it. But, the pain still showed on my face. At last, Edward finally called, and it seemed like I immediately had a reason to smile again after hearing his voice. Edward told me he would be home tonight and we would talk about everything that we had talked about the night before. When talking to Edward he seemed to be in a good mood, and actually seemed happy to hear my voice, and that too made me happy. However not knowing what he was going to tell me I just had a very good feeling about what he was going to say to me, but at the same time I had in my mind what Tammy Ann said to me from talking to her earlier.

As usual, I got the house chores done and was preparing dinner for Edward when he got home. I went and took my shower in hopes he might tell me what I really wanted to hear. I even went and put my make-up on so I would look good for Edward, and not look like I had been crying all day. I could hardly wait to finally get some answers, either way things went, I knew I would get my answers. I knew if he told me this was coming to an end I could get on with my life. Even though I knew it would take me some time and I would be extremely sad and very depressed for a while but I would eventually be able to move on. If he told me we could start a life together with a commitment, I just knew I would do everything within all my power to be a great wife and do, as he would want me to do. I loved Edward so much; I never planned on falling in love with Edward. I was not happy with how he had treated me early in our relationship, but I was willing to put all that bad behavior behind me to start over with Edward if that is what he wanted. I just knew he loved me, but I really believed he just did not know how to love the way I did.

My only concern was whether or not he would be willing to treat myself and my children better than he had. My head was racing with all sorts of thoughts and was wondering what he actually was going to say. I was getting so nervous, and very impatient waiting for him to get home. Finally, just as he'd, promised he came home right after work, and came in with beer of course, but this time was different he did give me a hug and a kiss. It made me feel like he was going to tell me that he too wanted to start over and give me the commitment that I wanted.

When he came in, I did not push for my answers. I gave him time to unwind from work, and as usual, he had to drink his beer before eating. I knew he had an alcohol problem as my daddy had when I had been a child. I drank with him in order to show him that I was willing to do what he did to make him more comfortable. When I was growing up I remembered my daddy drinking and promised myself I would not be an alcoholic. After his beer, he was ready for his dinner. And, just like before I received no thank you from Edward. I had kept quiet up to that point about the things that were weighing heavily on my heart. It seemed like he was doing everything he could to avoid having to talk about why he was there.

After he ate his dinner, he said he was going to go and take a shower, and then he and I would sit down and talk about what needed to be discussed. So, while he was taking his shower, I cleaned the kitchen up, then, went, and got his dirty clothes, and laid him some clean fresh night clothes out to sleep in, and also laid his work clothes out for the following day. I was so in love with him I even put toothpaste on his toothbrush for him for when he got out of the shower. After doing all of that, I went and sat on the couch and waited patiently for his answers. It seemed like he was in the shower forever.

Finally, he came out and he sat next to me. Edward said he loved me and we could get engaged, and would eventually get married. After he said that I was so relieved then I asked him, where we were going to live? He then said he owned four acres where his single wide mobile home was located. Then he told me that he wanted to buy a bigger home for me and my children. We could put it out behind the single wide and rent it out while we lived in the bigger home in the back. I asked Edward what we would do with my home. I couldn't understand why we couldn't just pay my house off and live in it, instead of trying to buy another house. He said he did not like the location of my house. I said that he had never complained while he had been there with me the last fourteen months. He then tried to tell me it was because he didn't like the neighbors that lived behind me but I knew the real reason was because he didn't like Tammy Ann and her family. I hesitated but agreed.

     I got to thinking that if I rented it out my house I would have something to fall back on in case something bad ever happened between Edward and I. Then I thought that Jordan might be interested in renting the house and paying the mortgage on it for me. The next day when Edward left to go to visit his friend, whom I never met, I talked to Jordan about my idea. Jordan was so excited and wanted to do it. He understood that he would have to have roommates in order to be able to afford the mortgage and I agreed to that. I felt good about it because I knew Tammy Ann wouldn't be far away if he needed anything. So, when Edward came home I told him what my thoughts were about Jordan staying in my home and having roommates. When I told him this, he immediately started complaining about my son.

     Edward flat out told me that he would not abide by my decision to let my son stay in my home. He said that if I decided to defy him that we would be through. It seemed to me that no matter how I tried to satisfy Edward and my children it was a no win situation for either side. Edward said he wanted me to sell my home and that my children were welcome to move in with us at the new house but that he would not allow them to stay in my home. Jordan made it very clear to me that he was not going to live with Edward. When I told Jordan I was going to sell the house, he was so disappointed. I felt like I had let him down in a major way. At the same time, I understood what Edward was saying about Jordan. I knew Jordan was running with the wrong crowd and some of his friends were doing things I would not want in my home. Jordan was young and liked to party and do things I did not approve of, and if he did not pay the bills at my home, I knew they would fall back on me.

     So, at the time I thought I was making the right decision, however, Jordan's heart was broken. Jordan moved in with a friend he worked with because he was not going to move into Edward's home because Edward had too many rules that Jordan could not live with. He was already over the age of 18 and considered an adult but Edward refused to treat him as such. However, Meghan said she would move with me, but she too was very unsure about Edward but she wanted to be with her Mother.

     After the decision was made, the hardest thing was to tell Tammy Ann, she to was very disappointed in my decision she told me she thought I was making the wrong decision. But, Tammy Ann understood how much I loved Edward. Tammy Ann could see that Edward did not love me the way I loved him. Tammy Ann said to me, "Michelle you are doing all the sacrificing and he is doing none. Edward has lived in your home for fourteen months and has saved all his money and now wants to buy another home to go onto is property." Then Tammy Ann asked me whether or not he going to put the new house in both of our names. I could not answer that question. Then she told me, "Michelle all he wants to do is get you back in those woods where you will be totally isolated, and where you would have no one and no one would be allowed out to see you."

     What Tammy Ann did not understand was that I felt like I did not deserve any better treatment. Tammy Ann knew that I had a low self esteem problem, but she always told me I deserved better. To me, her marriage was like a Cinderella story and I knew in my heart that I would never have that. So, I settled for whatever I could get.

     Edward and I started going to different places and looking at different houses, we finally decided on one and to my surprise he bought the one I wanted. That made me think we were finally on the same page in our relationship. I felt like he was trying to please me. After finding the house, I told Tammy Ann and she was extremely surprised. She even said that she thought he might be really trying. The house buying experience made us both feel more at ease with the whole situation.

     Edward bought our home in June of 2009 and I sold my home in the same month. Before we were going to be able to move into the house it was going to have to have a lot of repairs done to it. Edward decided to buy a repo house because it was much cheaper than buying a brand new one. The house cost Edward around thirty-two thousand dollars, and that is just about what he had saved while living with me. Just as Tammy Ann had predicted he only put the house in his name. That really bothered me because it made me feel very insecure, as usual. By Edward doing this it made me feel as if this relationship did not work then I would have no home to go to because I sold mine, but I tried so hard to believe in him that he would not do that to me. So, while the "new" house was being worked on we lived in his single wide with my daughter Meghan. My son Jordan lived with a friend from work and my oldest son was living on base at Camp Lejuene.

I had very nice furniture and so went ahead and moved all of it into the double wide. While Edward was at work during the day, I was at the double wide working on the house so we could move in. I spent hours cleaning the home, and trying very hard to hurry up and get the house ready for us to move in. In order to move into the home, the home had to be inspected and had to have water and underpinning underneath the double wide in order to get electricity, and the plumbing also had to be inspected in order to get electricity. We had to get a septic tank and run water about three hundred feet from where the road was to the home in the woods.

I had much work to do to get into this home. When I sold my home the proceeds I made from my home went right into his home, which I thought of as our home. I actually thought things were going to be finally good, I went and got new carpet for this home because the carpet in the house was beyond repair, it had so many stains on it even after I tried cleaning it. The walls were all white, also very dirty, and very nasty, so I cleaned all the walls, and then painted them myself. I also went and got all new toilets to go into the bathrooms because those to were so dirty and stained you could not get them clean. I also purchased several ceiling fans with lights to make the house look better.

Then while he was at work, I hired a friend of mine to dig a trench so I could lay pipe to get the water from the road to the house. It was a rainy day, I was so sick, and laying this pipe was over three hundred feet, because of working so hard my MS was flaring up. None of my work was ever appreciated. I never even got as much as a thank you from Edward. When the septic tank got put in he was two hundred a fifty dollars short and I paid that, and he never gave me the money back. I only got disability due to having MS and that was not much. So, as I was fixing the home up I was starting to see I was spending all my money and he was not spending none of his to fix this home up which was suppose to be our home. When I would bring this up to him he would get very angry and said we do not have to move into that home right now and that I was rushing things.

I asked him if that were the case why you even bought the home. I did not like living in his single wide. It was way too small and before even moving into his house, I had cleaned it from top to bottom. Edward had been a horrible caretaker. There had been dishes in his sink that had been there for over a year. They had mold all over them. In his master bathroom, he had been using his big bathtub for his dirty laundry. I also found dead mice all over everywhere. Of course, he ever appreciated my efforts. Edward was a very lazy person and did not take care of his home or his vehicles. He acted like he didn't even want to have anything better. I was the very opposite, I wanted a clean car and a clean home and to him those things did not matter.

When Edward came home from work, the first thing he would do was get a beer out of the refrigerator and drink till late into the night then he would finally eat his dinner. Edward's clothes were always washed, I always bought the groceries, I cooked every night, and dinner was always prepared when he got home. Edward would come home and his routine was the same every night: drink, play on the computer, and then talk about his job that I could care less about. But, when it came to talking about real issues like our life or dreams of our life he never wanted to talk about things like that. He never showed me any affection or showed me that he loved me. He would not even give me a kiss me after having been gone all day. I always kept my feelings to myself because when I would bring them up it would make Edward very angry. So, I learned quickly not to even say anything.

Chapter 9 Finally moving into our home

It was approaching October, Meghan was going to get her driving license, and I would put her on my car insurance. It was going to be an extra cost for me and I was getting absolutely no help from Edward. My soon to be husband was the type that he did not never want to spend one dime on me or my children. He would always say that he had not made the children and so he was not responsible for them. I often asked Edward whether or not he wanted to be a better step father than the step fathers he had. When I would ask him this question, he would never say anything, but would give me a dirty look. I learned very quickly I could not depend on Edward for any financial support even though I had spent most of my money on the house we were going to share once we got married.

Still there was more work to be done to the double wide before we could move in, and while Edward was at work I did all the work to get this home ready to move into except for the plumbing part. Before we could get electric, we had to put underpinning on the bottom of the home, to be able to get electricity. So one rainy day again me and my best friend, Tammy Ann's soon to be son-in-law helped me put the underpinning on the house, which to I had to pay him for his help. Of course, Edward never even offered to pitch in any money for the job Travis and I had done. Travis and I worked so hard that day and the ground was never leveled so it made it much harder to put the underpinning on the house.

As usual when Edward got home he had something negative to say, and that was also not appreciated. Because of the work Travis and I had done we were finally able to get electricity. I painted all the rooms and decorated them like it was a doll house. I even helped with putting hardwood floors down and replaced all the carpet. The house looked completely different than the day Edward had purchased it. I was so proud of the house and kept it so clean, the refrigerator was replaced and it was so pretty. The house was like what you might find in a magazine. I worked so hard on this home. Travis and I even cleaned out the woods in front of the house so I could decorate in front of the home and trimmed the trees because it was so ugly the way it was. When Edward got home and saw what we had done he through a fit and got very angry. He told me that this was his house and that if I were going to do anything to it that I would need his permission.

In November of 2009, we finally moved into the house. All of the furniture was mine, and it was decorated just the way I wanted it. I truly believed this would be the home I lived in the rest of my life. So, the money I spent on this home was not just for me but for Edward as well. I even sewed pretty curtains for our windows, which made them sentimental to me.

As we were preparing to get married, I just knew that after the marriage Edward would put the house that I had worked so hard on in both of our names. So, I never questioned him about it. I also assumed that we would share banking accounts together, like most married couples do. I wanted to get married in the mountains, so I looked online and found this very pretty marriage chapel, we did not want a huge amount of people just our immediate family. So, I also paid and made arrangements to get married in March of 2010. My parents were married on March sixth and that's what I wanted as well. I tried so hard to connect everything in my life to my family, the family that hurt me so badly. I wanted them to be so proud of me and when I finished decorating the house and we moved in, I invited them to come and look at it. My Daddy did come by once but my Mother never came. That also hurt my feelings and as usual, I felt badly about it. All my life I just wanted my Mother to love me, so when I told her that Edward and I were going to get married on the same day she and my father had been married, I just knew that would make her happy. I even sent out invitations to all my immediate family and did the same on Edward's side of his family. Edward did not want to invite any of his friends, I could not understand why at the time, and I did not even ask. I invited Tammy Ann and her husband Brent to come so she could be my maid of honor. And, of coarse she did accept she and her husband agreed to come. Where we lived and where the marriage chapel was in the mountains was about an eight hour drive and Tammy Ann was very OK about that because she loved me very much and loved our friendship.

The ring I got came from me allowing Edward to claim my daughter Meghan on his taxes so in reality he did not purchase my ring my daughter did from him getting money back from his taxes. Edward did not even split the taxes he received which were in my name and his as well, he deposited all of it directly into his account alone, and this was an account I could not get no money out of it because it was only in his name. I got very upset about that and told him I did not think it was right that he would not split the money with me, and again it was another argument, and one I never won. I knew what Edward was doing was wrong but I loved him so much and I for sure did not think I deserved any better.

As the time of our marriage was approaching I found out none of my family were going to come, except for my children and Tammy Ann and her husband Brent. When I found out my family was not going to come it hurt me so badly because of all of my marriages not once did they ever come and I did want a real wedding this time. All I wanted was for my Daddy to walk me down the aisle just once like what every little girl would want in her life. So, once again my heart was broken and again all them bad feelings of my life for so many years just flooded back of me not being a good daughter, a good Mother, or someone they did not even love or even want to know the person I have became. When my siblings did not come it hurt me as well, I was not surprised that Debbie and her family did not come or even want to come however by my brother Joe did not come that really hurt me even deeper because I actually thought we had more of a relationship than that. Then in my mind I would think of the wedding my parents did for my sister Debbie and they could not even come to mine to see me get married just once. Given I know I had already been married several times already but they never attended any of them and to me this particular wedding was the one that was special, the one I wanted so badly.

When I asked my parent's why they did not want to come, my Mother gave me the excuse of she could not travel because of her back, and reminded me of all the back surgeries she has had in the past. I pretended it was all right, however my eyes filled with water, from the hurt. I never allowed them to see the water in my eyes, because then I knew they would see once again how they were hurting me. So, after asking my parent's about this and then getting my answers I soon went home, and on the way home I kept thinking about the other trips they had taken far away from home and it never bothered my Mother's back doing that. I then knew it was just me, they did not want to do anything I needed them to do, or how I was begging them to just have something to do with me. All the way home I just cried, feeling as if I was nothing to them, and thinking just how much they did not love me at all. Feeling angry inside once again and soon as I got home, I called Tammy Ann as usual, telling her my hurt. As usual, she reminded me of how they were, but when she would tell me those things, it did not make me feel any better. So, when I got off the phone with her I would call each of my children, and they also would tell me the same things that Tammy Ann said to me. Calling all that loved me, just wanting some comfort, never made me feel any better, if anything the words each would say would only make me feel even worse. My children would get so angry with me reminding me of every situation that they have hurt me during my life especially Justin. My middle son Jordan had more affection to me and my feelings, he would always say to me "Mama I am so sorry that you have to feel that pain" when Jordan would say that to me I knew he was very sincere, he hated seeing me so sad.

My children have been there for me during their and my whole life, when I was not able to walk due to me having MS, my children would take care of me, bathe me, cook for me, and make sure I would have the medication I needed, like a small child. I felt like a burden to them but when it came to me, Justin, Jordan and Meghan we were so tight, and had so much love for one another. I was particular in cleanliness, and so was Jordan them small children would clean the home, do the laundry, and keep everything in order while I was sick so often in my life. I was so very proud of each of my children and the love I had and still have for them is something I told Edward he could never replace himself because my children would always come first. My children were my first priority and I often told Edward that he was not as perfect as my children nor would he ever be. The four of us were just that, they were my family and so many could not understand that and especially Edward. He resented them terribly, and never did anything for them and never shown them love whatsoever. I often asked myself how could he love me and not love my children because they were part of me.

March was approaching and it was approaching very quickly, so because of my Daddy not walking me down the aisle, I asked my oldest son Justin. I also asked Justin to wear his military dress blues, Justin was in the Navy, he was a Corpsman, and I was so proud of his achievements. He had already served a tour in Afghanistan, and the good Lord brought him home just in time so he could do this for me and also when he wore his uniform Justin was so handsome. Justin really did not want to do this but because I asked him and the love he had for me, he agreed. None of my children cared for Edward at all and nor did Edward care for them, however Edward was a grown man and my children were just children, and all my children had in their lives was just me. That annoyed Edward so much and being in his forties, he was so jealous of just children, and the love I had for each of them.

I often said to Edward why would not he want to be a better step-father than what he had in his life. When I would ask him this I never got an answer, except for an ugly remark such as "Michelle don't you think it is time you to stop breast feeding them". The thing Edward did not understand is when I raised my children, they were all I had and I was all they had nor did he ever want to even try to be a step-father. Edward hated my children because I always put my children first in my life instead of Edward. I just paid him no mind, because there was nothing he could say that was ever going to change my mind, especially when my children did way more for me than what Edward ever did for me. So after living in the home for four months, that I cleaned, decorated, replaced carpets, toilets, replacing ceiling fans, and painted the whole home it was time to get married. I went and got Edward's clothing he was going to be married in, and made all the arrangements for this date, without any help from Edward monetarily or even emotionally. We had moved into the home in November, so I could have my children there for Thanksgiving, and when I contacted my parents about this date they told me I could come to their home however they said my children could not. That did not set well with me because since being a Mother to these precious children, I never went anywhere that my children could not go to. If my children could not go then by all means I would never go. I could not understand why my parent's would say something as that, and I knew deep in my heart that for sure was not a Christian thing to say or do, however all my life I was use to them remarks however, my children were not. So, that is when I decided to just have Thanksgiving at my own home, which also irritated Edward. Since being a Mother to my children, my parents have never been Grand-Parents to any of them. My Parent's have never seen any of my children born including Angel, but they loved Angel but hated the others. Justin, Jordan and Meghan never understood them nor did they ever want anything to do with them because of how they treated me, when they treated my children that way my children really did not care because my children felt as they were evil people and those precious children did not want to even see them at all. Even when I tried to explain to my children, how Edward was, and even how my parent's were and still are my children said to me so often it just was not even fair or the Christian thing to do.

I knew what my children were saying was correct but I always tried to fix every situation. My children would get so angry with me for doing that, but I was only trying to do the right thing for everyone. When Christmas came and my children came to Edward and my home that I worked so hard on, I wanted a real family Christmas, a Christmas I always wanted in my life, with a family of my own. That did not work either; Edward never helped me get the groceries that I needed to prepare for dinner, to have a perfect dinner. Edward knew I had spent all the money I had gained from selling my grill, and selling my home to go into what I thought was going to be our home. All I had was disability for income due to me having MS. I tried so hard to make that check stretch, because Edward was so tight with his money and to him my needs did not matter.

Edward never talked to his Mother, and the only time he seen or talked to his Mother was only on Thanksgiving and Christmas, and he always had to go to her home on these holidays even though he knew I busted my tail to prepare a wonderful Christmas dinner for my own children. However, before having that dinner with my children we had to always go to his Mother's home even if that is not what I wanted. I hated that and did not ever understand that. I asked myself often why Edward would want to only go to her home just on holidays, and never during the year. Edward never even called his Mother on her birthday and if it had not been for me, she would never get a call or a birthday card with a gift card in it that always came from me, not Edward. When it came to Christmas presents Edward never got anyone anything including my children or even his own Mother. I had to do all of that as well but when I bought Christmas I always included Edward's name on the presents even though I did not like that and he never gave me any money back for this. As usual Edward would always have people to think this was all him, he always wanted to take the credit for everything, and put me down so often.

When Christmas morning came the first thing we always did was go to his Mother's house even after he knew I did not like or want that. All I wanted to do was spend this special day with my children, the children that I only had during my life, and that is what my children wanted as well. So, when I did this because of Edward go to his Mother's he would stay and stay even after he knew I wanted to go home and be with my children and celebrate this day with them, as what we always did since my children being in this world. Edward always got his way and if he did not, he would act like a two year old and throw fits, cursing and raising cane. Edward had a way of making everyone miserable and he liked it that way. Finally, we left his Mother's and I was so excited. I was able to be with my children, eat with my children, share gifts with my children and just spend time with them and be a Mother to them, something I loved doing so much. Usually after dinner, we would open gifts, and the children even being grown they acted like little children just wanting to open the gifts that they saw under the Christmas tree. Each of them just kept looking at that Christmas tree while they were eating their Christmas dinner.

After dinner, each of the children would help me clean the kitchen while Edward went to the computer, not socializing with any of us, just playing his games, as if Christmas was no big deal whatsoever. That really hurt my feelings because since being with me this was the very first Christmas we celebrated together as a family, so I thought. Justin was finally home from serving a tour in Afghanistan, so I really wanted this to be very special especially for Justin. The whole time the children and I were eating dinner that I had prepared, Edward had already gotten into his alcohol. Not just, liquor but also beer and to my surprise he had taken some of my medication, so to say the least Edward was feeling no pain. Edward went to my room and got him my xanax, something I had needed since Justin had gone to Afghanistan, worrying so much and praying so hard Justin would make it home safely.

Finally, the children said are we able to open our gifts? They all sat on the floor with me, except for Edward. I passed out gifts one after another, and even Edward had so many gifts under the tree and I would pass them to Edward. When I did this all Edward would do is just roll his eyes, not caring about this whatsoever because he hated that my children was in the home, and made that quiet clear to me from the very beginning. The more Edward would drink, the more hateful he would become. By not celebrating with us, not socializing with us, not even reacting or talking to us, even my children bought him presents when he bought my children nothing, knowing he had many of thousands in the bank. As I was passing the gifts out, the only gifts I received was from my children, he could tell I was so hurt, but continued sitting at that computer. I cleaned all the paper up trying as hard as I could not to show my emotions, but it was obvious the pain showed in my face because my children would just hug me and say they were so sorry.

I just hugged them back and saying to my children it is all right. I was so shocked though; I just knew I would of gotten a ring because Edward and I were about to be married. I was so very disappointed thinking how cruel can he be. Eventually Edward went into the kitchen, got another shot of liquor, and went outside. My children were so mad at him, and were talking about him to me while he was outside asking me all sorts of questions about Edward. Especially Justin, because Justin had always been so protective of me, even as a child. As we were talking, Edward finally came in and he had a bag in his hands that was from Zales Jewelry, my eyes lit up and I was so pale in my face and my heart was beating so fast. As I was opening the bag, my hands were shaking, and then I saw a box. I thought to myself he did get me a ring. I was smiling so hard. Just knowing I was right and knowing this would make me so happy. So, I sat down on the couch with all eyes on me, and when I pulled the box out of the gift bag something told me I was wrong about the ring when I saw Edwards expressions, but I tried so hard not to think about that. I started opening the box and when I lifted the lid I saw a necklace, not a ring, I smiled and said Thank You. My children knew me well enough to know that what he had done was even a bigger slap in my face than me not receiving anything. Edward knew he had done wrong, by the looks he received from my children, and the soft Thank You he had gotten from me.

I was not happy at all. And my reaction only fueled the fire in Edward and he started drinking even more, started acting ugly, talking ugly, and sneaking in my room and taking my medication without my approval, or me even knowing that he was taking my medication. As the evening was coming to an end, I tried with all my might to be happy and put on a happy face that I have done for years. My children have seen that look for years, and they knew I was hurt and because of that look, my children wanted to leave. The children were leaving and were going to go and spend time with their friends, I hated to see them leave, but I knew why they were leaving it was not because of me it was because of Edward. However, I could not blame them at all, and wished I had a place to go as well. As they were gathering up their gifts to leave, each of them hugged me and said "Merry Christmas and Momma we love you." Each of them were so sorry for the actions of Edward, and what he had done to me made the children not to like him even more, but because each of them knew just how much I loved him they did not say anything to me about him. When they finally left none of them said one word to Edward or even wished him a Merry Christmas.

Chapter 10 The fight on Christmas

My kids were leaving and I knew that Meghan was preparing to back to Georgia the next day. With only one more day at home she said to me, "Momma I will be back to see you tomorrow." I said that would be great and then she asked, "Mama will you cook me some chicken and pastry?" I said I would be very happy to do that for her. Justin and Jordan overheard what I said to Meghan and said they would also be with Meghan to come and eat the next day. That made me extremely happy knowing my children would be back the following day. I loved being with my children, we would always talk about the past, and laugh at some of the silly things that we had done together while they were growing up. When I went back into the house, I told Edward that the children would be back tomorrow to eat chicken and pastry. I could tell by his expression that he was not happy at all, but he did not say anything He knew that even if he had said anything I would not have cared.

When I told Edward about my kids, he started drinking heavily. Then he became loud and verbally abusive. He started talking about my children and all of the mistakes they had ever made. I knew that he had made many of the same mistakes that my kids had but he would never admit to it. Edward never wanted anyone to know that he had gotten in trouble from having drugs and also from having two DWI's. Edward would always say that he had gotten himself out of jail without anyone's help. He would not admit that his Mom had been there to help him all three times. Edward wanted everyone to think that whatever he had or had done, he had done or gotten on his own, which I knew was a lie.

Especially the house we were living in. I knew the reason why he was able to buy the home we were living in was because he had lived fourteen months in my home not paying for one bill and on occasion he would just buy just a few groceries. Edward would just keep talking nasty, putting my children down, and calling them names that were so uncalled for. He just assumed that I would keep taking it. As he became more and more drunk, and high on drugs his behavior only got worse. Eventually, I had finally had enough. I told him what I was thinking, which included him using me. I told him how he always took from me but never gave me anything in return. Then I told him to shut up. I finally went into my bedroom and shut the door so I could isolate myself from him and his trash talking.

In my heart, I knew what he was trying to do and that was for me to distance myself from my children. When I went into the bedroom to get peace from him, his language, the dirty words, and how he stated he hated my children, I just cried. I kept asking myself what I have done. Why did I give him all my money by putting into this house that I mistakenly thought would be our home? Edward had me over a barrel, and he knew that. Everything that Tammy Ann had said to me was coming true. While I was lying on the bed in another room, I still could hear him cursing, and raising cane the entire time. I got the remote control and turned the volume up on the television, trying my best to drown out the words that were coming out of his mouth. I had the bedroom door locked so I thought he would not enter, to my surprise he tried to come in and me locking the door, only made him madder and then he kicked the door in. Then I knew all Edward wanted to do was fight, fuss, and argue with me and this was all because my children came to be with me for Christmas.

Edward was so jealous of the bond my children and I had and still have to this day. All the actions he did after my children left only get worse. He was continuing to drink even more, I went into the kitchen where the alcohol was, and I saw he had consumed almost the entire bottle of liquor and when I opened the refrigerator, I realized he had consumed most of the beer that had been the fridge as well. Edward also had been into my medication as well but I did not know that. I knew this was not going to be a very good Christmas for me at all. I still was carrying all of the pain that I have had during all of the past holidays in my life while raising the children on my own and by not being able to spend this time with my Mother, Father, and especially Angel. All of these thoughts kept racing in my head of all the past, all the holidays I missed with my precious daughter Angel, the hurt I carried for so many years. When I tried talking to Edward about all of this, it only made him more furious and he made me feel like what had happened in my life was my entire fault. I held my head down as usual knowing I couldn't argue or even try to talk with someone that was as drunk as he was. I learned this sad fact from having grown up with my father. He just continued to tell me what a terrible person I was and what a terrible person I had been when I was younger. Then Edward called me a name making me feel as I was nothing more than trash, pointing out to me that I have had three children by three different men, as he was saying this horrible thing, he then thought of Angel and then said no not three children but four children by four different men. Edward knew just what buttons to push to hurt me, and when he mentioned Angel's name I began to cry, and felt the pain once again of the loss of my precious daughter. Edward would just feed off of my pain and by him seeing my pain; he only got worse with his behavior. As I continued crying, he only drank more, and more, and by him, seeing me cry the words that came out of his mouth only got worse and more hurtful. Edward brought up everything of my past, as he was doing this I thought about my Aunt in Georgia, when she told me when I was younger about never sharing things of my past, and she told me if I did this then the very people that you love will always throw them hurtful things up in your face. My Aunt told me you may love them with every fiber you have but they will not love you the way you love them, and by them knowing your past all it would do if you told them your past is them people would use that information as ammunition against you when an argument would take place. My Aunt was right because every time Edward and I would argue, which was very often, Edward would always throw up my past and also throw up my children and their behavior in my face. I could never understand why he would throw up my children because my children never did anything to him, except try and be nice to him because of me. My children knew I loved him but my children also knew he did not love me the way I loved him, however Tammy Ann along with my children just tolerated him for me. I knew I had a problem and have had that problem all of my life, I would try to buy spouses, friends and many others so they would like me, the problem was me not liking myself, from so many putting me down including my own family. My brother Joe is a minister and he has also used my mistakes in many sermons he would preach about in his church, if he would only know how this would hurt me, and never would he ask me how I felt about him using my mistakes and naming my name in his sermon.

When he would do that I just wanted to find a hole and get into it, from shame, from hurt, and mostly how could my own family continue hurting me, when I loved them all so much. So, when Edward would do what he would do, it was just like my family would do. All of my life, I felt like I deserved this behavior from others. Edward's tirade went on for hours, and it was beginning to snow, which was something North Carolina did not get very often and especially on Christmas day. Instead of this being a wonderful day that I had planned for many months turned out to be the very worst night I had experienced for many years. Edward's behavior brought back so many terrible memories of the Christmas's I had during my life.

When my children were small all I had with me during this special holiday was just my children, it seemed like all I have ever had in this world was my children. It was so sad, especially when they were small and wanted to know why they did not have Grandparents like other children. I had no answer but deep down I knew why my parent's did not want me or my children there at their home during the holidays and it was because of Angel, they did not want Angel to have any kind of relationship with us what so ever. They did every thing they could do to distance her from my little family. As Edward was continuing his ugly behavior I went into the kitchen and just stared out the kitchen window, leaning on the kitchen counter watching the snow fall, with tears flowing down my face, asking God when is my life going to be better? Asking God when will I ever have a family that is complete? Asking God when will I ever have a someone that feels my pain, feels my hurt, talks to me, someone I could trust, pleading to God what have I done that is so bad that I had to have a life like this?

As I was in the kitchen leaning on that counter Edward came in and told me to stop feeling sorry for myself, but never asking me why I was so upset. Edward then got another drink and then he proceeded to get even drunk, if that were even possible. Soon things got even worse and he got in my face like my father used to do when he was drunk. I could smell the awful stench of alcohol and could feel the spit on my face as he yelled. I asked him to get out of my face and that seemed to only make him angrier.

I was just so thankful my children were not there to see what he was doing to me. They would have been furious and probably would have beat Edward for having upset me so bad. He was so drunk at this point that he could no longer walk a straight line. He was staggering and banging up against walls and when he tried to use the toilet all he succeeded in doing was making a huge mess. When I confronted him about it, the horrible behavior was amplified. Edward became very aggressive the cursing became more violent and when I asked him not to curse, he informed me that he was in HIS house and could do whatever he wanted. He then proceeded to tell me that the house would never be mine and that my children were not welcome. Edward then said that I would never have a place in the house that I had spent all of my savings fixing up. I tried to tell him that this was not just his house but was mine as well. Immediately, Edward became physical. He even went into the bedroom, got his handgun, and started waving it around.

When Edward did that it scared me so much that I called Justin and told him what was going on. Edward heard me calling Justin and he became even more violent. The reason I decided to call Justin was because all of his life, Justin had been my protector. He was the one when he was little that was the man of the house and the one that would never put up with his Mother being abused in any kind of way. Edward heard me talking to Justin, telling Justin what was going on, and telling him I needed him. Edward grabbed the phone from my hand and told Justin if he came out to the house, he had something for him. I instantly knew what he was talking about. I started screaming and I told Justin not to come.

After Edward hung up the phone, he got back in my face and told me he dared any of my children to come to his home. Then he started hitting holes into the walls, the walls I had painted in the house I had worked so hard on to make so very nice. Then Edward saw me again leaning on that counter looking outside watching the snow and crying. The counter was next to the kitchen sink and next to, the flat top stove that I loved so much. When Edward saw me crying again then he came into the kitchen and put a hole in that wall as well. Then he banged his fist on the flat top stove and the flattops just shattered into pieces, and when I tried turning the stove on to see if it would work it would not do a thing. He had smashed the stove because he knew my children; especially Meghan wanted me to make chicken and pastry the next day.

I was so heart broken and not only that I now feared for my life. I knew what I had to do and that was to call the police. While I dialed 911 for the police to come, Edward became even more furious. This is when he told me he did not love me, nor did he want me, and wished I would go somewhere else with my children that he hated so much. As he was telling me all of this, he was continuing putting more and more holes into the walls of the house. While he was punching holes in the walls, he was also telling me the only person he has ever loved was a woman that he was with over twenty years before I came into his life. When he told me that he had never loved me, my heart fell to my feet. My face turned so pale, my pulse was racing, with such fear. Finally, when Edward knew the police were on the way he went and put his handgun away, even though he was drunk he still knew what he was doing even though he claimed he did not know what he had done.

When the police came then, were two officers and they came in the home, and were asking me all sorts of questions. I showed them the holes, the broken stove, and told them how he had been treating me but as I was telling the officers these things Edward was sitting into a chair in the living room, acting as if he had done nothing wrong. When the officers asked Edward what had happened he told the officers that it was his home and if he wanted to punch holes in the walls or even break the stove then it was his business because Edward said these things are all his property. I could not believe him. I was the reason he had all of the nice things he had. I even told the officers about the gun, and then Edward said he was only checking the gun and making sure it was clean, so the officers did nothing, the officers said he had every right to break anything that belong to him since this was his house. I could not believe it; they were not going to do anything, while I was thinking they would at least take him to jail from being so intoxicated from so much alcohol.

When the officers left, I became very scared and that is when Edward told me to find some where else to live, and he did not want me at his house any longer. I asked Edward were was I going to go, that I have spent every dime I had into this house that I thought would be our home. Edward said nothing, and eventually he passed out from all the alcohol he had consumed. I was so relieved that he had finally fell asleep and was hoping so much that he would not wake up until all the liquor was out of his body. When Edward went to the bedroom and finally fell asleep I knew I would not go to bed with him, and stayed up all night fearing that he would wake up and do something harmful to me.

The next morning after a sleepless night, I was trying to figure out how I was going to cook for my children. When Edward finally emerged from the bedroom, I did not even speak to or even look at him. I had so many different emotions flowing inside of me that I was sure he did not want to know what I was thinking. When he came out of the bedroom and went into the living room where I was, he did not even know what to say to me, but how he was acting I knew he wanted to say something to me but he did not. Edward immediately went and got his keys to his truck and he left, I had no idea where he was going, and I did not even want to know where he was going. I was so ashamed that I had to call the police, and the things he said to me the night before. Edward had no idea how he hurt me, and to me I did not think he even cared. However when Edward left I was so relieved, hoping he would stay gone forever. I cried and cried and all the hurtful words he had said to me and him not willing to even talk about what had happened, knowing I had no one to even talk to about this.

I just prayed and asked God why? All I have done since being with Edward was to show him just how much I loved him. I had done everything I could to fix the home we were going to share, even sewing and making all the curtains in the home, panting the walls, decorating every room so that when people would come and visit they would think the home was a doll house. I asked why would he want to destroy something we bought and why would he want to destroy what I had worked so hard on? All of this was so confusing to me, he told me he loved me but his actions told me much different.

While I was trying to clean up his mess before my children were due to come later for lunch, I was wondering what I was going to tell them about what had happened. I knew my boys would not appreciate what Edward had done to me. I also knew that they would loose any respect they had left for him over this ordeal. When all these thoughts were flowing threw my head, my cell phone rang, and it was Edward. When I saw Edward's name appear on my cell phone, my first reactions was not to even answer the phone from feeling such pain that he made me feel.

Reluctantly I gave in and answered the phone and the first thing he said was do you want white or black? I asked what he was talking about. Then he asked whether or not I needed a new stove. I said yes, but then I said that he knew that we talked about replacing it with one that would match the refrigerator. I also told him that I wanted a flat top like I had. Edward said of course, you always want the most expensive one they have. I then said that I hadn't been the one to break the stove and because he had, he should get the one I wanted. I also informed him that I was not going to help him pay for the new stove. He then informed me that he had not asked for my help and he understood that he had broken it and so he should be responsible for replacing it. Then I said Edward when you get back home with the stove I think we need to have a very long talk. He said nothing to that as usual. When it came to talking, Edward would talk about work and other people, but he would never want to talk about our relationship. It was something I could never understand. Edward loved talking about work, and that was something I else I could not understand. Edward was an electrician, and I knew nothing about that. If you wanted to talk, about house cleaning, cooking, and other things like that I could understand those things, but were topics he never wanted to talk about. I never in my life knew what conduit were until I met Edward. And, that is all I ever knew and all he wanted to talk about. To Edward talking was talking about work, never talking about our relationship or how we could improve it, to me we could never connect the way a relationship was suppose to.

When I thought about this, it reminded me of my childhood, because that was the only thing my parent's ever did. They would talk about their job, and nothing more. I remember at the age of twelve I probably knew more about Guildford East than what most people did that worked there. As a child and as an adult I did a lot of thinking, never forgetting anything that crossed the path of my life. Edward and my relationship, reminded me of my parent's relationship. They never talked about their feelings for one another. The only thing they had in common was work, and Edward and I did not even have that. I knew nothing about electrician work, and he knew nothing about my life or the work I had done.

While Edward was gone in the snow that we had gotten the night before, I thought of all of this and kept asking myself if this was the way it was going to be if we did continue with our plans of being married? While he was gone, it gave me peace that he was not there however I had no clue how I was going to explain all of this to my children that were due to come later in the evening. I did not know if I was going to have a stove or whether or not I would be able to prepare the dinner that my baby girl, Meghan, wanted so badly. As usual when I had something on my mind I just leaned on that same counter as I always have done in the past. My leaning caused calluses on my elbows that were so ugly.

Eventually, Edward came home, and as he was driving down the dirt path, I noticed a great big box in the back of his worn down truck. When Edward came in, he said to me, "Michelle I got you a stove, and one I hope you like." As we were taking the broken stove out of the house, my children showed up and wondered why we were replacing the stove. When they asked I tried so hard not to show my emotions, but they knew something had happened between Edward and myself. So, they started asking me questions all I could do is tell the truth, and by telling the truth that only made things worse, especially when it came to my boys Justin and Jordan. My children were not even there five minutes but they knew they did not want to be there any longer, because they wanted to say something to him so badly.

Because of me and because I asked them not to do that they said, "Momma we love you, but we do not care for Edward at all and we cannot stay here with you while he is here." My children begged me to get away and not to marry him. Justin said "Momma you used to be the strongest person we had ever known but since being with that drunk you have gotten soft and have allowed him to do you so dirty." Then he said, "Momma you have done everything for him." After that, he asked what Edward had ever done for me besides put me down. Justin then said Momma, "Don't you think you deserve so much better than what you are getting?" Deep down I knew what Justin was right, and little did Justin know that Edward was taking every ounce of power away from me, making me think I did not deserve any better. Something I had gotten use to in my life from so many, my family, so many spouses, and now Edward.

Edward did get the stove I wanted which was a stainless steel stove to match our refrigerator. While he was bringing the new stove into the kitchen, I asked him what we were going to do about the holes that he had punched into the walls the night before. Edward then asked me to let him do one thing at a time. I told him that looking at those holes reminded me of how badly he had treated me the previous evening. He then asked, "Michelle, just what did I say?" I asked him if he was sure he wanted to hear all of it. He replied yes I want to hear it all. I said Edward you called me terrible names from having four children by four different men. Then I said to him he said he wished he was with the girl he was with from twenty years ago. When I told him these things, he said there was no way he would have ever said anything like that and that I was wrong. I said Edward I swear you said it and then you got your gun and was waving it around. I told him how scared that made me feel. After telling him everything that he had done, my eyes were filled with tears and my face showed such pain and my heart was broken.

Edward never said he was sorry for hurting me but he did tell me that he loved me. To me they were just words, and they were words I did not believe. Later that evening I called my children and told them I had made some chicken and pastry and for them to please come and eat some, and telling them I made this dinner just for them. The children came but they for sure did not want to come especially knowing that Edward would be there while they were there. The children and I stayed in the kitchen while Edward was in the living room playing on the computer, and not saying one word to my children. Edward's behavior reminded me of when I was a small child and my parent's got into arguments. It also made me feel like I had to walk on egg shells, so I was sure that is how my children were feeling. After my children and I ate dinner we often would play cards with one another and we all asked Edward if he wanted to play, he quickly replied no and continued playing his games on the computer. Edward did not talk at all which was really fine with me because at least I was feeling peace, because as long as he did not talk I did not have to hear all the ugly words that came from his ugly mouth and behavior. The children and I played for several hours then they decided that it was time to leave; I hated the thought of that because as long as my children were there Edward did not do things that were so ugly.

After my children left Edward then started drinking again but this time before it got so out of control, I went to bed. I was still not getting any of the answers for the questions I had asked him before. Edward never wanted to apologize for anything, and since knowing him; he has never apologized for anything even when he knew he was wrong. So as usual, I never got any kind of answers from Edward about his past, about the present, or even about his behavior. Edward showed me no love but told me he loved me, this confused me so badly, but I knew I loved Edward but I was so confused if he loved me however he told me he did, then he just said he did not like or love my children. That bothered me so badly because how could Edward love me and not love my children.

The morning after the police had been called, he said he did not remember any of the behavior he had done, he said he did not say or do the things I had accused him of, and that I was delusional. Edward had a way of making everything my fault. He would never stand up as a man should and take responsibility for his wrongs, or his behavior, or his ugly words he would say about my children or to me. So, trying to talk to Edward was like going down a dead end road. Edward saw in my facial expressions how he hurt me during this holiday that I wanted to be so special, he ruined it all with my daughter coming from Georgia, my son finally being home from Afghanistan, and Jordan coming to the house as well. It had been several years since we were able to have a Christmas once again together. All I wanted was a Christmas that my children would see how much different things were now than what they had as children. Just having a complete family, having a soon to be husband, and for them to have a step-father, just having a complete family. A family was I had dreamed of for years.

My birthday was approaching and still I did not have a ring. Knowing that we were going to be married in less than three months, I did not think I was probably going to get one. I for sure did not think he would get me one for my birthday. At the beginning of the New Year I allowed Edward to claim my daughter on his taxes, even though this is something my daughter Meghan did not want, however he told her he would give her some money from the taxes, so after he had made that comment to her, she was fine with the decision. The necklace I had gotten for Christmas came from me putting three thousand dollars into his account from the house that I sold, to make a home together. That really hurt me because if I had not of done that, I knew I would of never even gotten anything for Christmas, Edward was as tight with his money as a bark on a tree. This hurt me and it hurt deeply, to the point that the necklace I received for Christmas did not mean anything to me at all because that necklace was bought with the money I had put into his account. So, when Edward got his taxes back the check was in both of our names, however, he gave me none of the money. He deposited all the money into his own checking account, an account I could not even touch.

Needless to say, Meghan did not receive any money from it either. This hurt me, not to mention how it hurt my daughter, and when I brought this up to Edward this would only make him very angry making him say he is not her father, and he did not make her and he would not be paying no child support for children he did not make. Many of the things Edward said were completely so self centered, and so selfish and all about himself. So, the day came and it was my birthday, he said let's go to Jacksonville and gets your birthday present. I really did not want to go and the reason was because whatever he would of gotten me for my birthday I knew what I would of gotten would of came from the tax money that he did not share with my daughter Meghan nor did Edward share with me. This made me very upset, that when it came to my birthday in January, I truly did not want anything from him at all. I was still completely still upset about his behavior during Christmas and still not getting and apology to me nor did he apologize to my children from his behavior and the horrible words he called me and my children. However, Edward still claimed he did not recall any of these things. I knew deep down he knew what he had done and all my life I had always heard that when someone was drunk, that they always spoke exactly what they felt. Those thoughts played over and over into my head, as so many thoughts have before. I have always had such terrible thoughts in my head, and these thoughts would never escape, wanting them to go a way so badly, they never did.

As we were preparing to leave and get my gift, this did not mean very much to me, because the money he had gotten from his taxes was going to pay for my birthday present. So, as we were heading to Jacksonville, it was so quite in the vehicle, neither Edward nor I said anything to each other. This forty-five minute drive felt as if we were driving hours, I was so unhappy, so confused and we did not talk about anything he had done at Christmas. Months before Christmas, I had seen on television this beautiful Everlon collection that was white gold with such a beautiful diamond in the middle and had a rope diamond figure around it meaning that the rope will never let you fall. This collection was so pretty and one that I wanted. However, I wanted it but I wanted Edward to pay for it with his own money, not the money he had taken from Meghan or me. For Christmas, I did receive the Everlon necklace and it was very pretty however, what I really wanted was the ring for Christmas, and did not get it.

Edward knew this hurt me badly so for my birthday he was trying to make things right by getting me the Everlon ring to match my necklace. I wanted a matching set but how I got it made me not want it at all. When it came to Edward's ring I had to also pay for that as well, which I truly thought I should have not had to do that since I had paid for all the plans of us getting married in the mountains. This marriage cost me thousands of dollars and I asked Edward to help me and when I did that he responded by saying the bride's family is suppose to pay for the wedding, and Edward knew I had no family to do that and he knew the reason why. Then I said Edward the groom is suppose to pay for the honeymoon, and explained to him that the package I bought from the beautiful wedding chapel in the mountains already paid for the honeymoon, so I asked if he could help me on that. Immediately his response was no.

However the package came with a wonderful cabin, a wedding cake, this cabin had an indoor swimming pool, a hot tub, a wonderful loft, a kitchen, a deck that had a grill on it so we could grill out if we decided to do that, it was just perfect and so pretty. The view that this cabin had was breath taking, something I loved so much. So arriving to our destination to get the ring I wanted I could tell by Edward's expression this was something he did not want to do, but knew he had too. When I talked to him about getting married and asked him if this was something he really wanted to do he stated, "Everyone should do it at least once. " When Edward said that to me, he had no idea, how those words were so painful. It made me feel so very unwanted and to me those words were so powerful, and so heart breaking but from years before I had learned to hide my feelings so well, putting on a happy face, acting again, as I have done so much in my life so many times before. The necklace and ring was something I had wanted, however I wanted it from Edward, not the money he paid it from, and taken away from me and my daughter Meghan, I thought that was so spiteful, so selfish, and very hurtful.

As Edward and I went into the store, to get my birthday present, we saw the rings and the Everlon, collection. Edward did get me the ring that I wanted however in my heart that the ring did not come from Edward it came from me or my daughter Meghan. I did not say anything but I had to admit it was very pretty on my hand. I was very happy about the ring and the Everlon set that I had gotten, however I was completely disappointed in how I received it. In Edward's mind, he thought all the money he had received was due to him, he thought everyone owed him something. I asked Edward why he wanted to marry me, and asked him if he loved me. Edward did he say he loved me and I asked him how did he love me? When I started asking him questions of these things it would make him uncomfortable or it would make him upset. Following asking him these questions he then said to me I was a good cook, I was a good housekeeper, and I was a good painter. I thought to myself, WOW! Is that all Edward could say about me and then I asked myself is that the only reason he wanted to marry me?

Chapter 11 The weekend of our marriage

March of 2010 was approaching, and approaching very quickly, and I was gathering all the things we needed for the major event that was getting ready to occur in my and Edward's life and that was to become as one by getting married. As I was gathering all the clothes and packing the suit cases and all of the other things we needed, I was thinking and talking out loud to myself. I kept telling myself that this marriage was going to work; I told to myself that I wanted to marry Edward. I did not like some of his ways and especially the fact that he drank so much and the way he treated me while drinking. I thought to myself that if he truly didn't like my kids and didn't really love me like he would tell me when he was drunk then why he was going through with this marriage.

Trying to please my parents, like I had done all my life, I wanted to be married on the same day they had married on and this day was March 6th. I have been married many times and so I thought I was becoming the next Elizabeth Taylor but instead of my last name, being Taylor it was going to be Price. When I said Michelle Price, it just did not sound good together. However, the name Michelle Molsen sounded even worse. As every bride would do, they would write their new name over and over just to see how they would write it, and how it would look, as you would write it. In my case, any last name was better than what I was born with.

Several days before Edward and I would be leaving to go to the mountains Tammy Ann and I went and got Edward a wedding present, so I could give to him after the wedding day, so I could give this to him the night of our honeymoon. The only people coming to our wedding was my best friend Tammy Ann, and her husband Brent who took off from work to come to my wedding because they were my very best friends. Also my children Justin, Jordan and Meghan also came, Justin also brought a girlfriend of his and that was fine with me as well, so they were the only people on my side that were going to come to my wedding, the dream wedding I had always wanted. Tammy Ann kept all her negative feelings about Edward to herself however I knew just how she felt about him and how she did not like how he treated me in such ways that were mental and emotional abusive behavior towards me.

On Edward's side, he only had his sister and his Mother to come, and to my surprise he did not even invite anyone else but not knowing that when the day came to get married. Tammy Ann made sure I had something blue, something borrowed, and something new, Tammy Ann was such a planner, and she always did things in order. When you would go into Tammy Ann's home, you could see just how much hard work she put into her home. Her husband Brent was a truck driver and while he was on the road, Tammy Ann made sure the yard was cut; the house was remarkably clean, and decorated so pretty by Tammy Ann.

Tammy Ann also cleaned all the vehicles that they owned. Tammy Ann and Brent had a marriage that reminded me of a fairy tale, Brent would and did do everything for his wife, he was so supportive, so loving towards her, and I never ever heard them argue about anything. Tammy Ann and Brent always put their family first and were such great parents to their children even if they messed up. I was hoping so badly that the marriage Tammy Ann and Brent had would be the marriage Edward and I would have. Tammy Ann and Brent's marriage was as if it was a fairy tale something like a Cinderella story. Their love towards each other was so obvious and something I was so jealous of and hoping that one day Edward would see how Brent treated Tammy Ann that he would learn from Brent then eventually learning from Brent that he would start treating me the same way Brent treated Tammy Ann I was hoping.

As we all were heading to the Mountains which was over an eight hour drive, we all drove each of our own vehicles, Edward and I drove my red Monte Carlo SS because the cars Edward had was not very dependable, and especially not dependable enough for that long of distance. Edward worked four days a week, working ten hours a day, so he was always off on Fridays, and also off on every weekend, Edward only took one day off for our marriage, so by doing that he would not have to go back to work till Tuesday the following week. Tammy Ann and Brent drove their family truck, and the children all rode together to save on gas because the children did not have a great deal of money to spend, and they only came because I wanted Justin to walk me down the aisle in his dress Blues.

Finally, we got to the mountains and Edward and I checked in the wedding chapel where we were going to be married the following day, and then they gave us the key to the cabin we would be staying in for two nights and three days. Edward and I had gotten there first, and when we went to the cabin that I had paid for including me paying for the wedding. The cabin was everything that the chapel said it would be. This cabin was so beautiful, it had the in ground pool in the basement of the cabin, It had a hot tub and a grill on the back upper deck, and the view of the mountains was so spectacular. I was beginning to think this was going to be the wedding that I have always dreamed of all my life. Even Edward was very pleased of what I had been done to make this an event that neither he nor I would ever forget.

After Edward and I looked at all, the rooms Edward said he was going to go to the store. I asked him what he was going to the store for and he replied he was going to the store to get beer. So, I unpacked our clothes and hung up my wedding dress in the closet, and also hid the wedding gift I had gotten for Edward to give to him after we had got married. When Edward came back to the cabin not only did he have a case of beer, he also had a fifth of liquor as well. Immediately I started thinking of the Christmas we had just a few months prior, and the Christmas I had to call the police on Edward, and all the ugliness that had taken place during that holiday. While I was thinking all these negative thoughts my cell phone rang and it was Tammy Ann and she said her and Brent had finally made it. Tammy Ann told me she and Brent had rented a motel room about four miles away from where Edward and my cabin was. As Tammy Ann and I were talking, she asked me if something was wrong, and as usual, I said no. However Tammy Ann knew me all to well to know that I was not telling her the truth, but I did not want Tammy Ann to know what Edward had done by buying all that alcohol, when we were suppose to be getting married and enjoying one another.

I just wished Edward would of not have done that, and that is when I knew Edward was an alcoholic, and if he was awake he was going to drink, the same as my father did when I was a child. I also remembered what my father said to me about Edward, he said "Michelle if you mess this relationship up with Edward, I will beat your tail" my father did not know Edward really; he for sure did not know the Edward I knew. My Father did not know how Edward put me down and mentally and emotionally abused me and said horrible things about my children. While talking to Tammy Ann on the phone I was thinking about all of these things, questioning myself a whole lot of not marrying Edward, knowing several people had come to see this event, and I did not want to let them down. I was feeling I was making a huge mistake but at the same time, I was thinking who else would want me. So while on the phone Tammy Ann asked me when the children were going to come? I said they would be here in the morning of the wedding. Then Tammy Ann asked me when Edward's Mother and sister were going to arrive. I told her they would be here in just a few hours. Then she asked if Edward and I were going to eat dinner with Edward's mom and his sister, I said no because they would be getting in too late to eat dinner, and besides Edward did not even call his Mom to even see where she was or when she would be in the mountains. Edward never had a good relationship with his Mom except for Thanksgiving and Christmas, and that was the only time he seen his family during the whole year. So while still being on the phone with Tammy Ann, we decided that she and Brent would like to go out and eat with us, so while on the phone I asked Edward if that would be all right with him, reluctantly he said alright.

Edward really did not like my best friend and thought her husband was a wimp because how he treated his wife Tammy Ann, how good he was to her and how he treated and loved her. Edward did not agree with all of that and said to me that Tammy Ann is spoiled and it is because of Brent. When Edward would make those remarks, I would just ignore him. Edward was never happy with anyone and to me he did not like any one. Edward never smiled, and never seemed happy, and who ever was around him he made sure they were not happy either. I just could not understand why he was the way he was, however like most women they think they can change men or change people. Tammy Ann and I agreed that we would meet in an hour so we could get ready and Edward and I would meet them at their motel room.

As we went and got into the shower to get ready to go out with Tammy Ann and Brent, I could tell that this was something Edward did not want to do because all he wanted to do was stay in the cabin and drink his alcohol. When I was taking my shower, he was already drinking, and after I finished taking my shower and getting my clothes on I told Edward, he could go ahead and get into the shower. From his ugly expressions, I could tell he was already feeling the effects of the alcohol; however he did as I asked without trying to start an argument, which was a surprise. As I laid his clothes out to wear to go out and eat, he asked me to go and fix him another mixed drink. When he asked me to do that, it made me feel really bad, because instead of celebrating us getting married he thought this occasion was more of a vacation than a wedding. So after us getting ready and getting ready to meet Tammy Ann and Brent he had to drink one more mix drink before leaving, when he did this it made me feel so badly.

    We finally left and met Tammy Ann and her husband Brent at their motel room and we went to a wonderful steak house. The food was great, and so was the company; however you could tell Edward was really ready to go. I knew the reason why, but I would not share this with Tammy Ann. I am sure she knew already because she knew me so well that she began to read my facial expressions very quickly and knew what I was thinking. Eventually the waitress finally came with our bill, and a bill I knew would be high because Edward had ordered so many mixed drinks and it sat on the table. As always when Edward and I would go out and eat, I would always have to pay the bill. Tammy Ann and Brent knew this and because of me telling Tammy Ann they knew I had paid for the complete wedding including the honeymoon without any help whatsoever from Edward. It made Tammy Ann and Brent very frustrated with Edward, so Brent grabbed the bill and told me this was my wedding present from him. Brent and Tammy Ann were and still are such great people, and Tammy Ann would do anything in this world for me which only made Edward hate them even more, Edward always thought I got my ideas from Tammy Ann which was totally wrong, I had a brain, and I had my own thoughts without anyone telling me anything. I knew just how Edward was and how bad he acted and treated me without anyone telling me how he was. We finally said our good byes at the restaurant and said to each other we will see each other the following day, which was going to be my wedding day.

    As I was thinking about this wedding day I just knew things would change after we got married. As most women think, we think things will change or think maybe you can change them, but in my case, Edward always made me think it was me that needed to do all the changing. As Edward and I were heading back to the beautiful cabin that I rented for this very special occasion, we went and got into the pool, and as usual he continued drinking and drinking more alcohol. After swimming in the basement pool, we decided to get into the hot tub that was on the upper deck. The whole time doing this there was no affection, no talking about our wedding day that was going to take place on the following day. After getting out of the hot tub, I called my children to see what time they were going to be there because the time that we were going to be married was going to be one o'clock and I wanted to make sure they were going to be on time. I pleaded with Edward to call his Mother but he refused to do so, he said Michelle she knows where the chapel is, and she knows what time the wedding was, but I thought why he would not call his Mother to see if she made it alright, and to see if she made it safely.

    I knew why I had such negative thoughts about my family but I did not understand why he had such negative thoughts towards his family. Edward would never talk about it either. Edward did not even call his father to tell him he was getting married, and I did not understand that either. However, I knew by asking him all these questions would only make him angry and more furious about the wedding, because he did not want Tammy Ann and Brent there either not to mention my children. Edward was a loner he did not have many friends, nor did he want any. If Edward was on a deserted island and if he had food, a computer, and his cigarettes and especially his beer he would be just fine. He never wanted to talk about any issues except the issues about money, Edward loved money and that is something he loved most in his life. As we were preparing to go to bed, he was so drunk that he did not even tell me he loved me, did he hug me, or did he even kiss me good night. I went to bed feeling so lonely even though lying next to me was Edward.

    This affected me so badly that when I finally went to sleep I woke up around one in the morning feeling so sick. I thought that the sickness feeling would go away but all of a sudden, I jumped up and got sick in the bathroom, not even waking Edward up so he could help me. Then the sickness only got worse, not only was I throwing up, I also was having sickness at the other end as well. This sickness kept getting worse and even more badly, all in my head was how I was going to be able to get married tomorrow with me throwing up and having sickness at the other end as well. This went on all night and at this time, I was not a Christian, and was not able to hear what God was telling me, but now I know all to well what God he was telling me. I was sick because this was a marriage that should of never of taken place. Eventually Edward woke up and I was so sick, and he saw how sick I was and he went to the store to get me some sprite and other drinks that should have made me feel better. These drinks did not work, and I was so thirsty that when I would drink, I would drink and drink, and as soon as I would drink these drinks, the sickness from both ends would happen again.

While I was in the bathroom again, throwing up my toes Tammy Ann called and Edward told her I was sick. She then asked about the wedding. Then Edward asked me whether or not I was going to be up to getting married. I told each of them that, yes, I was still going to get married today. I was a fighter, and someone that wanted something so badly I would find some way of getting this done, however God had other plans and I did not know that. Being the friend that Tammy Ann was she was at the cabin quickly, and about the same time, Tammy Ann showed up so did my children. I could barely answer the door without getting sick, and after unlocking the door for everyone to come in; I immediately went to the bathroom and got sick again. This time sitting on the commode and having the trash can in my hands to throw up in it. I was a complete mess.

When Tammy Ann saw me this way, she told Edward when he returned with more sprite and sport drinks, that he needed to call this wedding off because I was barely able to walk, was continuously throwing up. She suggested that I needed to go to the hospital and then told him that I was dehydrated. So Tammy Ann called the wedding chapel and asked them if we could marry the following day due to me being so sick, they said yes however it would have to be late into the evening. Tammy Ann told them that would be fine.

By having to do this I knew Tammy Ann would not be able to see me get married or be my maid of honor because Brent had a load, he had to get somewhere the following day on his big truck. So, Tammy Ann and Brent had to leave, which disappointed me greatly. Edward's Mother and sister had to leave as well because Edward's sister had to go back to work the following day. The whole time we were in the mountains Edward did not even see his Mother, which I thought that was really disrespectful. I thought Edward should have at least gone to see his Mother and his sister at the hotel they were staying in. However, it did not seem to matter to him what I thought. Edward did exactly what he wanted to do.

When my children arrived, they told me they did not have any money to rent a motel, and asked me if they could stay with Edward and me in the cabin, and of coarse I said yes. That made Edward mad, and the children saw this, but Edward knew better to say anything to them especially because I had paid for all of this myself. Then Jordan came to me and told me they needed money to go back home on after the wedding, because they did not have much money at all, and the money they had went towards the gas to come to the mountains, so I gave them money as well, and this too made Edward mad. Instead of Edward taking care of me, my children took care of me, just as they have since being in this world. By Justin being a Corpsman in the Navy he told Edward as well that I needed to go to the hospital and told him as Tammy Ann had told him I was dehydrated, but Edward said that I would be alright in a little while.

I was not all right, even though he had bought me some nausea pills. I just continued throwing up, sitting on the commode, and having a trash can in my lap. This was so bad, and I had never been as sick as this my whole life. Since one o'clock in the morning till seven o'clock at night, this is all I did. Eventually Edward knew I had to go to the hospital, and on the way to the hospital, we had to stop often so I could throw up outside of the car. It seemed everywhere I had gone with Edward it always turned out to be a nightmare. We eventually got to the hospital in the mountains, and as I went in I was throwing up and even they could tell how sick I was. Because of the nurses, seeing how sick I was, they immediately got me in the back so I could lie on a bed. For that I was so thankful because I was so sick I could barely hold my head up, and that was because Edward had waited so long to carry me to the hospital.

That also made Tammy Ann and my children so angry, and showed them things I did not see or maybe I just did not want to see of him not loving me the way I loved him. When the Doctor came into my room she said to me, we have to put an IV in you that you are terribly dehydrated and need IV liquid desperately. As

Edward was leaving the room, that Doctor asked me if I felt safe at home. I could not understand why she would ask me this, but I told her yes that I felt safe.

Chapter 12 The Ugly Truth

Edward stayed gone and I had no idea where he went, but he was not there for me when I needed him the most. This particular Doctor I had was a female Doctor and she kept asking me over and over if I felt safe at home? Because I did not know why she was asking me this particular question, I asked her why she was asking me that. I said Dr. Why are you asking me that question. Explaining to her today was suppose to be my wedding day and because I was so sick we were having to get married tomorrow, she did not even know me nor did she know Edward so I did not understand. But when I asked her that question of her wanting to know if I was safe at home, she replied back to me by saying he has a very bad look on his face. With her not knowing Edward, I explained to her that he never smiled, or is ever friendly to anyone. Edward was much like my Mother with no personality but I did not tell her why he looked so angry, but I knew why. Edward was angry that he had to take me to the hospital, and that interfered with his drinking, and thinking that the children were going to drink all of his alcohol. When Edward came back into the room and seen that I had an IV hooked up to me, which only made him more angry, and then he said I guess we are going to be here all night.

When Edward made that remark it made my eyes fill with water as if he did not care, this remark hurt me so badly. Once again, I thought I was trash, and he could care less about my health, or what had made me so sick. As they were running all sorts of test on me I could see the look in Edward's eyes that he had no love for me the way a husband or soon to be husband was to feel towards their wife or soon to be wife. While I was lying there in that hospital bed Edward kept leaving and not staying with me when I needed him so much. I needed his comfort, I needed his support, and I needed his love. All I knew if the tables were reversed I would of never of done Edward the way he had done me. Then thinking all these negative things, I kept asking myself am I doing the right thing by marrying this man tomorrow. Could I teach this man about love? Could I teach this man how to communicate with each other besides just communicating about his job, or how he hated my children? My head was racing with all sorts of thoughts, and I was so unsure about everything. Then I would think about the time when I was a child and how my own Father would drink, would Edward be able to stop drinking the way my Father eventually did? I had so many questions and really wanting to talk to Edward about these questions but Edward was not the type of person that wanted to talk about real issues. Doing so made him very uncomfortable, and made him get upset that he would use such ugly words to the point it would hurt so bad, so I thought the best thing was to be just quite about all of it, knowing deep down I wanted so much more.

Wanting a marriage like what Tammy Ann and Brent had, but knowing what they had was a Cinderella story one I thought I never deserved. As I had talked to Tammy Ann so much about this she told me many times that I deserved way more than Edward, and I deserved a man that would love me as much as I would love him. Just lying there in that hospital bed thinking about all of this made me just cry even more. Laying there crying and all sorts of thoughts running through my head, such as me selling my house, and because of me selling my house my children no longer lived with me. It was something I missed so much, but the reason they did not live with me now was because of Edward and his behavior and how he would talk to them. Edward thought he could tell them what to do when he had never been in their life while being a child, my children were all grown at this point and my children had no respect for Edward whatsoever. Also by selling the grill, and my home and all of the proceeds I had gotten went into Edward's home leaving me broke. Only being able to support myself on disability which was not enough for me to get a place of my own so my children could come back and live with me, Edward knew this and this could not of made him more happier.

Edward knew he had me over a barrel and knew I could not go any where else. Edward had thousand and thousands of dollars in the bank, and when it came to me he would never give me anything. If he ever did let me borrow from him I always had to pay him back as soon as I got my disability money. While I was lying there in that hospital bed, I felt such grief, such pain, and thinking I did not deserve any better. I had always promised myself I would never be with a man that drunk alcohol as my Father did when I was a child. It seemed as all my dreams, all of my wants, and all that I needed in this world was not ever going to happen. While raising my children, I always would think of the day that I would be a grandmother and how I would be such a great grandmother to my grandchildren, but I also knew Edward would never allow me to be able to do any of that, because of the hatred he had towards my children.

I thought about all of the holidays we could have as a family that would mean so much to me. I dreamed about all of the ball games my grandchildren would have and me attending to support them as I had done for my children. I dreamed of going to their school and eating lunch with them on occasion, me buying them gifts to surprise them once and awhile, just being the very best grandmother I could be, because my children did not have that in their life, all they had was just me. As I was crying I asked myself why does he feel such hatred towards my children, what has my children done to him to make him feel such bad feelings towards them. If anything, my children tried so hard to show him he was now a part of our little family and even told him the quote we had, and the quote went as this "We are strong, we are tough, and we will always stick together."

When my children told him this I remember the look Edward had on his face and later Edward told me that quote was just crap, something that only black people would say, when he said that I thought how cruel can a human being be? I lay there thinking about all of these things and wondered what I was going to do. Wondering how could I survive just on disability, and knowing deep down I could not live on my own just on disability, especially after I had spent everything I had on Edward and on the home he said that would be ours. I was stuck once again not having a place to go except Edward's home, a home I knew I would not get to see my children unless Edward was at work or out of town due to his job.

I lay there thinking about all of this, and thinking what in the world have I gotten myself in to. As I was lying there and crying the Doctor came back in and once again, she asked me if I was safe at home. I did not know how this Doctor knew what a cruel of a person Edward was and how ugly he could be at times, but again I said yes I am safe at home. Edward acted very different when he was drinking alcohol, but when he did not drink alcohol he was a much nicer person. While lying there in that hospital bed, I thought about the beginning of mine and Edward's relationship.

How on Friday and Saturday nights coming home late after closing the grill how he would have my tub filled with a hot water filled with bubble's ready for me to have a relaxing bath and him cooking on the grill so I would have something to eat. I remember how things were so much different then what they were now. Edward would hug me, and kiss me and lay on the couch with me and watch television with me after working such long hours. Edward knew I had MS and by having this terrible sickness, he knew my legs and feet would hurt terribly, and by knowing this he would rub my legs and my feet making them feel so much better. In the beginning of our relationship, we would talk, and play cards, and we laughed and had a good time together as long as we were alone but when others were around, and even when my children were around us he would act completely different, by doing this he was not the Edward I fell in love with. The Edward I fell in love with would show me such affection, and made me feel such love without having to ask him to.

Now the Edward I know I would have to beg for his attention, even having to ask him to kiss me or even hug me. I often wondered what I had done to him that he began treating me so differently than what he did when we first got together, then I would ask myself, if he felt that way then why in the world would he want to marry me? While Edward was gone from the hospital room I was in I was wondering if I should marry him the next day or not, thinking about the very beginning to now. How Edward lied about the girl calling him on Christmas Eve two tears prior and telling her he was alone when he was laying right next to me, then Edward doing a back ground check on me to find out everything about me. However, I barely knew anything about him, and then me spending every dime I had made from selling my grill and my home and giving him mostly all my proceeds that I had gotten. Then thinking how Tammy Ann and my children telling me how he had done nothing but uses me the whole entire time. Also thinking about the times we went out and ate and me even paying for that. Also when we would take a vacation such as the cruise, going to the mountains two times and the wedding me having to pay for all of these things as well while Edward paid nothing.

In reality Edward was the type that wanted to lay, play and stay but not ever pay. The home he had just purchased was because I allowed him to stay with me for over a year in my home and he paid nothing, and he was saving every cent he made, while I was completely broke, and when I did have money he had a way of taking that also. Edward was all about Edward and not caring about my feelings whatsoever. But my parents thought he was Mr. Wonderful but they never knew the things he had done to me or to my children, however, if they had known they would of not have cared. As Edward came back in the room where I was he had told me he went and got something to eat and he then asked me how much longer were we going to be there at the hospital there in the mountains? Not asking me how I was or if I was even feeling any better. I knew he was ready to go, and the reason why was where he could go back to the cabin and get to his alcohol, not caring how I was feeling or even not caring what was wrong with me. Now being a Christian I know now why I had gotten so sick, it was God's way of trying to prevent me to marry this man, and God knew I deserved much better. The problem was I was not a Christian at that time, and I thought I did not deserve any better than Edward. Now being a Christian, I know now Edward was nothing more than the devil in costume.

The hospital finally released me late in the evening, and gave me a few prescriptions to get filled while I was there. On our way back to the cabin we did get the prescriptions filled, but this did not make Edward happy either because it was so late many of the drug stores there were closed so we had to go to several drug stores before we found one that was open. Eventually we found a drug store that was open and we were able to get the prescriptions filled. All the way back to the cabin, Edward did not even say one word to me. He had this gloom look on his face and acted as if he was angry about every thing that had happened as if I wanted to throw up and become dehydrated and for having, a horrible day was my fault as if this was something I had wanted. As soon as we left the drug store and got back to the cabin, the children had already cleaned the cabin up and cleaning up all my mess that I had made from being so sick, with throw up all over the place, in the bedroom, in the bathroom, in the trash cans all through out the cabin.

When the children saw me they all hugged me and said "Momma we are so sorry that you are sick." It was something that my soon to be husband did not even say to me. After me, telling my children the Doctors could not tell me why I had gotten sick, and then telling them how I had to have an IV due to me being so sick and very much dehydrated. So, after telling them all that had taken place I then told Edward and my children that I was going to take my medicine and I was going to bed in hopes that I would feel better the following day. Thinking that Edward would come to bed with me and be more attentive towards me but he did not. I went to bed alone and he stayed up drinking till he passed out.

As I went into the bedroom of the cabin and getting my pajamas on I went out into the main room, and told everyone good night. When I did this, I noticed how Edward was watching my son's girlfriend looking at her from head to toe and especially her breast and her butt, this hurt me even more and when I tried kissing him good night he turned his head away and I was only able to kiss him on his cheek. I did not say anything about it because I did not want to hurt my son either and I had already been through enough for one day. As I was lying in the bed in the bedroom, I was listening to Edward laughing and joking with Justin's girlfriend knowing this girl was young enough to be his daughter and not to mention he was suppose to be marrying me the following day. Edward did not know I was in there listening to all that was being said, and some of the things Edward had said to Justin's girlfriend really hurt because he had never said them things to me or about me. I eventually feel asleep feeling no self worth, no value, or feeling any love whatsoever something I was all to familiar with in my life. I have been used, lied to, hurt by many including by my own family, and have gone through so much in my life having many other failed marriages and wondering if this one was going to fail as well.

The following morning after waking up I felt somewhat better but still not feeling as what I wanted to feel like, but as usual I was a great actress and I pretended to be much better knowing deep down I was still sick. I knew that we were due to be at the chapel at one o'clock that day which was March 7, 2010. This was not the day I wanted, I wanted to be married on the same day as my parents were married on which was March sixth. In hopes, my parents would like that, and still trying to do anything to gain their approval even as an adult. When Edward woke up he did not even ask me how I was feeling, nor did he act even excited about being married this day and this being his very first marriage, if any thing he acted depressed and very withdrawn and did not have much to say to any one that morning. As I was preparing breakfast something I really did not want to do, but the reason I did this was because I knew my children did not have much money to go and get them something to eat, so I prepared breakfast for them and them alone. However, Edward had to eat breakfast also, my children told me thank you for doing it, but never did I get a thank you from Edward. My son Jordan loved cooking at the grill and even enjoyed cooking at home when he was little when I could not cook because of when my MS would flare up. So, by my children knowing me all so well Jordan came in the kitchen and helped me clean up the kitchen.

After cleaning the kitchen up, I went back to the bed and tried to take a nap before the wedding. As I was lying in the bed trying to go to sleep, I could not go to sleep from all the thoughts that were racing in my head. Thinking about my past, thinking about my future, just thinking about all of my past marriages and all of the wrong choices I have made during my life, wondering when things were going to be different. I could not answer any of the questions that I was asking myself, which made me feel even worse than I was already feeling from being so sick. The time was coming quickly to get married once again but this time I prayed to God that what I was getting ready to do was doing the right thing even though I knew I was not a Christian.

So, I got up and went to the chapel salon so they could give me a terrific hair style and also did my make up. This was something I had never done for any of my previous marriages, and they made me look so beautiful that I could not even believe it. When I looked in the mirror I saw a person that I did not even recognize and was hoping Edward thought I was beautiful as well. When I walked into the chapel to meet Justin whom was going to walk me down the aisle, I noticed Edward sitting on the bench with his head laid on top of the bench in front of him. That made me feel like he was regretting this completely and acting as if he was making a complete mistake, which made me, feel horrible. When I saw the minister go to Edward and telling him it is time, Edward moved very slowly to the alter. Not knowing what to think by him doing this all I could think of is he either Edward had a hangover from the night before or Edward was regretting all of this and not wanting to get married. However Edward knew if he did not marry me, I would want all my money back that I had put into the home we were suppose to share and we could not just have a friend with benefits relationship. As the preacher was starting us both looked at each other and I smiled at him and he had no emotions on his face whatsoever towards me, his face was blank with no feelings at all. When I looked into his eyes as he was saying his vows, it was like he did not even know what he was saying, and even messed up and got it all confused that the preacher had to walk him slowly through the vows. As the minister finished with the ceremony, he announced this is now Edward and Michelle Price. As we all went outside including my children, it was time for pictures to be taken and each of the pictures Edward never smiled in any of them. To my surprise my son Jordan went up to Edward and said Edward welcome to our family, and Edward said nothing back to him, and as you can imagine that hurt Jordan's feelings a lot. As soon as all the pictures had been taken the children told me they were leaving because Justin had to report back to his base at Camp Lejuene the following day.

I understood however, I wished they could have stayed longer. When going back to the cabin I immediately called Tammy Ann and told her I was now a married woman once again, while on the phone with her she asked me how I was feeling? I told her I still did not feel good but I made it through the wedding and it was finally over. When I paid for the wedding, I also paid for the food that we would receive after the wedding ceremony. I had ordered steak, baked potato, and a garden salad; the steak was raw and was so we could grill it out on the grill. Edward hurried up and cooked the steak and we ate however I could not eat very much from still feeling sick from what ever I had the day before. Instead of staying in the cabin and spending time with one another, Edward wanted to go to the casino, which was over an hour away. I did not want to do this at all but to make him happy that is what we did.

As we were driving to the casino I tried very hard to talk about the wedding and instead of him telling me I looked beautiful, I had to ask him if I did. I asked him about my hair and about my make up and how good they did that no one that did not know would not know just how sick I actually was. Trying to make conversation was also very hard, because it seemed Edward did not want to talk at all. This all hurt me especially by not even commenting on how I looked for our wedding. I have never looked so good in my opinion, and my hair was so gorgeous. To me all it seemed was Edward was only thinking of himself by even wanting to go there to the casino after knowing just how sick I was, and how it seemed he did not care.

Chapter 13 The Honeymoon Night

When we arrived at the cabin Edward still did not hug me, nor did he kiss me, and the thing that hurt the most was Edward seemed as he was regretting marrying me already. When my children left they told each of us they loved us, and I told them I loved them also however Edward did not even say a word. Edward acted ugly towards them even during our wedding pictures. The camera lady was taking pictures of the family and Edward did not want to get close to any of my kids. She even asked him to get closer to me and the children because he was standing at a distance. When she asked Edward he looked at her as if he was disgusted with everything, and just wanted it all to get over with. So, he could do what he wanted and that was to go to the casino and start his drinking as he did each and every day since knowing him. As I was thinking about all of this, the only time I did not see him drink was the one time I saw him sick. He did not drink that day, but that only lasted a day.

So, after the wedding, we went back to the cabin where the food was so Edward could cook the steaks on the grill, and the baked potato, and the garden salad had already been prepared. Edward ignored that and did not want to cook or even eat a piece of the wedding cake. That made me feel so horrible, so unloved when I had just got married, I knew deep down I should of never of had to feel those feelings. I had paid for the entire wedding, the food, the cabin and all of the trimmings of this wedding even all of the photos that were taken. Edward had thousands of dollars but did not even ask me if he could pay for any of these things, Edward knew I only received disability, which was not a lot of money, while Edward had many of thousands of money in the bank. Edward was all about money and the more I gave and had nothing, the more he was able to save and never would Edward offer me anything to cover any of the expenses of our wedding, not to mention the other trip we had taken a year prior, and even the cruise I had taken him on. All of these things were again in my head, of how selfish Edward was, how the one love Edward had was the love of money.

On the way to the casino, we had no conversation with each other, it was so quite, and I still did not feel good whatsoever and could not understand why Edward would not just want to stay at the cabin. This was our honeymoon night and I just wanted to stay at the cabin and watch TV together, cook the food that had been bought and just spend time together, however what I wanted was something I did not get as usual. The drive to the casino was miserable not to mention it was over an hour drive there to the casino and an hour back to the cabin. I thought on the way of how Edward was so tight with his money I couldn't figure out why he wanted to go and spend money and usually when you go to any kind of a casino the odds of winning are not in your favor. This was something I could not understand that this was something that Edward wanted to do and especially losing money at a casino when he could not even give me any money to celebrate our wedding by getting a souvenir of getting me something I could always have to remind me of the day Edward and I got married.

I loved Edward so much; Edward was someone that I did not intend on falling in love with, however I had. I loved Edward hard, he was the center of my universe, and however Edward did not act the same towards me or my children. While we were driving to this casino in the mountains, I just stared out the window with tears flowing down my face. It was my wedding day and I just wanted Edward to love me the way I loved him. I wanted Edward to tell me he was so thankful that I was his wife now, and to be proud that I was his wife as I was so proud that he was my husband, but he showed no emotions whatsoever about any of this blissful event, that had just taken place. Before marrying Edward I thought things would change after we got married, and he would act different towards me once we got married. I knew the next morning we would have to check out of the cabin, but because I was so sick I did not enjoy that beautiful cabin, and that was another reason why I wanted to stay at the cabin instead of going to that casino.

We finally arrived at the casino, instead of him getting valet parking, we parked very far away from the casino, and I had to do a whole lot of walking. He knew how sick I was, but once again, I being the great actress I have had to be all my life. I pretended this walk was not bothering me when actually it was making me feel even worse especially him knowing I had MS, as well. While we were walking this long distance he did not hold my hand, nor did he wrap his arms around me, he walked several steps ahead of me, not to mention it was so cold in the mountains at March and if someone had looked at us they would think we were not even there together. This disappointed me extremely bad and for this to be my wedding day; Edward hurt my heart so badly. After paying so much for this wedding, the cabin, photo's and the food that I had paid for, I was not able to enjoy them days at the cabin, the cabin was wonderful and it was something I will never forget how I was done on this day by Edward. It hurt and it hurt badly, and I was so badly disappointed by his actions and his behavior and how Edward treated me.

    Once we got into the casino, I had no money to play any kind of casino games, nor did Edward offer to give me any. I had spent all I had on the wedding, and the extra's that came along with the wedding. So I just sat next to him, bored out of my mind and all the noise of the bells and whistles were so loud that the noise was giving me such and headache when I did not feel good as it was. Edward could tell by looking at my face and knew I was not having a good time. After he seen my look on my face he told me I was being selfish, and I was not allowing him to have a good time on his honeymoon night. So once again I put on this happy face, something I was use to all so well, but while I was doing this I was thinking just how selfish he was when he knew I was sick and all I wanted to do is stay at the cabin after we got married.

    I sat there and watched him spend and spend and him never asking me if he could help pay for the wedding. As I was thinking about all of this I would recall about all the other trips, we had taken and Edward never helped me pay for any of that as well. I had such a good heart and thinking about all of this to me it seemed as I paid for so much to just try and buy his love. Especially remembering the remark he said right before we got married sitting there watching him them thoughts were running through my head and that remark stuck with me that he said " everyone needs to be married at least once." Thinking in my head why would he just say that when I so badly wanting him to say "Michelle I love you and I want to spend the rest of my life with you." Anything like that would have been so special to me. I loved Edward so very much and would do anything for him, and did. I wanted Edward to love me as I loved him, but no matter what I did, was never good enough. All my life I have tried to please everyone, buy their love, even when I was in the second grade, I would give girls my ice cream money just so I would have friends. Thinking about all of this while he was sitting there putting in twenty dollar bills one right after another, and me sitting there with nothing, once again thinking about all of the things in my past to try and get someone to love me again.

    While being at the casino, moving from one machine after another following Edward and watching him spend so much money and not winning anything back, I just could not understand because of how tight he was with his money. He was having such a good time while I was completely miserable being there at the casino, he eventually asked me if I wanted to play. I said Edward I have no money, he gave me fifty dollars reluctantly, and I think the reason he gave me the fifty dollars was just to get me away from him. I did not like the slot machines that he loved to play, so I went to the blackjack tables. I loved blackjack and was quite good at playing that game. In no time, I turned that fifty dollars into almost four hundred dollars and that made me very excited. As I sat there at the blackjack tables without my new husband, a couple of hours went by, and Edward finally found out where I was. When he saw how much money I had won, instead of just asking for his fifty dollars back, he took all of my winnings. I completely thought that was wrong, but because he had lost so much money on the slot machines he felt as if I should give him all of my winnings to him to replace his loss. After doing that to me, that made me upset but once again I did not say anything. After taking my money that I had won Edward said he was ready to go, which was completely fine with me because in reality I did not even want to be there to begin with.

    All I wanted to do to begin with was stay at the cabin, in the first place. Ever since we arrived it, felt like I had been sick and I had not been able to enjoy the cabin at all. I had spent over three thousand dollars for this wedding, cabin, food, and much more for this wedding that I had wanted so badly. Edward was a man that I loved so much and once again in my life, I actually thought I could teach him how to love, not to mention teach him how to love my children. This marriage I wanted so badly and the very last marriage I wanted in my life. Edward was a dream comes true for me; he was so good looking, and never had been married before and did not have any children. When he and I took pictures together, you could see just how we looked so good together. I would have done anything in this world to make this marriage work even if it meant that I was unhappy, I loved him just that much.

On the way back to the cabin from the casino, Edward never even said anything to me during the long hour drive. Edward never told me how happy he was that he married me, nor did he hold my hand or show me any affection whatsoever. I was so disappointed in Edward's behavior but I knew he had been drinking at the casino and I just thought that was the reason why he was treating me the way he was. But I just knew after we finally got back to the cabin he would act differently towards me. Finally getting back to the casino, Edward did cook the steaks on the grill, but also during him cooking the steaks all he did was drink alcohol, the entire time. The salad was already made, and while cooking the steaks on the grill he also cooked the baked potato's on the grill as well, it seemed like it took him forever to cook this food since Edward had told me was such a grill master. Finally, he finished his cooking on the grill, and when he bought the steaks in, they were burnt, he made the excuse of the grill not cooking right, and the steaks were horrible neither him or I ate very much of the steaks, nor the baked potato's however we did eat the salad but while eating he was still drinking. I asked Edward if he wanted any wedding cake and he said not right now meaning he still wanted to drink more.

While he was continuously drinking, I lay on the couch and started watching TV thinking he would do as well, but that never happened. I was wanting so badly for him to show me some kind of attention as rubbing and stroking my hair, while I was lying on the couch. I wanted him to sit on the couch and allow me to lay my head on his lap and for him to play with my hair, and make me feel better and give me some kind of comfort from being sick. That never happened and I eventually feel asleep on the couch, and when I woke up, he was in the bedroom asleep snoring like crazy. So as I went into the kitchen and looking at all the alcohol he had consumed, I knew he had finally passed out and went to bed. I was so hurt, and very disappointed because this was a horrible honeymoon night for me, and it was all about Edward once again, he did not even try and wake me up, so I could go to bed with him. I went in the bedroom where Edward was and tried to wake him up, and he told me he was tired and wanted to go back to sleep, that night he did not even tell me he loved me or tell me he was glad I was his wife. I laid down next to him he started snoring again so loudly that I could not even go back to sleep nor did he even wrap his arms around me to hug me while we were laying in the bed together on our honeymoon night.

The only kiss I had gotten on our weeding day and honeymoon night was when the Preacher announced us man and wife, and that was it. I was so hurt and very disappointed once again in my life, and once again thinking what was wrong with me. Wondering if he really loved me or not. While those thoughts were floating around in my head and in my heart, I was wondering why Edward even married me to begin with. The next morning when we woke up Edward knew he had done wrong, and he also knew that we had to check out of the cabin today. So, while I was gathering everything up and loading things in the car, he knew I was very upset, I did not even talk to him and the whole time I was thinking this is just a great way to start off a brand new marriage between Edward and me. When Edward and I left the cabin Edward could tell I was very unhappy, and on the way of going to turn our keys in to the cabin, he asked me if I would like to spend some time in the town of Gatlinburg, the town where our cabin was located. I said sure I would love that, Edward was trying to make up from how he acted the night before however I knew if I had not won the money back at blackjack that he lost at the casino we would not be doing anything for our wedding, we would be going back home.

After turning back the keys from the cabin, we went to the town of Gatlinburg and parked the car and walked around, it was so pretty and I enjoyed it so much. I had always wanted to take an old time picture of old clothes back in the nineteen twenties; I just loved those clothes and often wished I was born back in those days. So Edward agreed to do this, it was fantastic and he bought me two pictures of us together in those clothes. Little things made me happy and as long as we were doing something together so I could have memories, those things were so precious to me. I am very sentimental and the little things he did that day made me very happy. Then when we were going to store after store I saw this nice sweatshirt with a hood that said Gatlinburg, and I liked it so much that Edward bought it for me. I treasured that sweatshirt so much because it came from Edward and as soon as he bought it, I immediately put it on and wore it all day. After getting the sweatshirt we then saw the high cable chairs that went to one mountain to another and I wanted to do that as well to just see the view, since I loved the mountains so much. As we got on the lift chairs and went up in the air Edward wrapped his arms around me and made me feel so good, Edward was a completely different person when he was not drinking alcohol, he was very loving and very kind to me as long as he was not drinking. I loved that part of Edward so much, when he was not drinking, and he treated me, as I was his queen and someone he loved very much. While we were on the chair lift, they took a picture of us together and it so happen to be the time he had his arm wrapped around me so tightly, and was showing me such love and attention. When we got to the top of the mountain and unaware they had taken a picture of us, that when I saw it and when Edward saw the look on my face Edward knew I wanted that picture so badly, and he bought it for me.

      After going down the mountain in the chair lift Edward gave me a kiss and told me he loved me so much. After that and from the night before of feeling sad and very depressed of how he treated me, he had made it all up, by how he treated me the next day in Gatlinburg. After that we decided to start heading home and I was really fine with that, we started driving back this long eight hour drive we stopped at different fruit stands, jelly stands and gathered a few more items. Edward was so nice that day and very affectionate towards me as he should have been the night before, however I knew I had to let them feelings go because he was really trying to be different this day. So in my mind I tried really hard not to think about the wedding day and what he had said about everyone should at least get married once, and how the casino went, and then him passing out on our wedding night.

      When we were about four hours from home, Edward asked me if I was hungry and I said yes, so when we got to Winston Salem we saw this place called the Olive Garden. It was an Italian place to eat and that was one of Edward's favorite foods to eat. We had a very nice meal and once again he was treating me like a lady and acted as if I was someone he loved very much such as opening the door for me. He did not walk in front of me but instead he was held my hand as we walked together and made me feel he was very proud that we were together. For the very first time I was, feeling loved, respected, and finally Edward made me feel as if he was so proud that I was his wife. I also was very proud that Edward was my husband and had told everyone that I was a friend with before we left that Edward and I were getting married. I thought Edward had done the same thing however later on in our marriage I found out differently.

      As we were approaching home and at the store about three miles from our home, he stopped to get cigarettes and beer. When I saw the beer, I again was disappointed but I did not say a word because I did not want to mess up the day we have had. As soon as we got home and unloaded the car he immediately started drinking the beer he had gotten at the store and as soon as he started drinking I seen a very big difference in his behavior once again. Edward did not help me unpack, or anything he just continued drinking and got on the computer playing his Face-book games. As I was putting the dirty clothes in the washer Edward yelled out "can you bring me another beer?" I said, "Yes," however, deep down I did not like it.

      As a child my Father was an alcoholic and I promised myself I would never be with anyone that was an alcoholic, then I felt like once again I just settled with another man that really did not love me but loved money and his alcohol way more than he loved me. After finishing putting all the stuff up from our trip, wedding, and getting the dirty clothes washed Edward had drunk a whole lot of beer. I called my children to make sure they had gotten home safely, and as I was talking to my children, they all three noticed something in my voice that they could tell something was wrong, however when they asked me I did not tell them. I just told them I was really tired and still not feeling good. I later got into the shower thinking that maybe this would be the night that we would make love as man and wife. When I got out of the shower, I then knew Edward was drunk again, and I knew I did not want to make love to Edward for our first time as man and wife when he was drunk. So I told him I was going to bed, kissed him good night, and told him that I loved him and he said OK. It hurt my feelings so much that when I told him I loved him that he did not even tell me he loved me back. As I got into the bed I recall crying myself to sleep wondering what in the world have I done? Why did I once again love someone so much and that person not loving me the way I loved him. As I was crying I prayed to God that things would be different and Edward would stop drinking every single day and just slow down on his drinking, and love me the way I needed to be loved, and to love me more than he loved his money.

Chapter 14 The First Two Weeks Of Being Married to Edward

The next day Edward had to go to work, and I was left home alone, feeling that I had messed up once again by marrying Edward because of his drinking, and how he loved drinking and money way more than he loved me. I knew I had to change all of my identification cards like my Medicare card; I had to change my driving license along with all my banking information. The following day I decided to go and get all of this over with, still not feeling good about my decision, however I did go ahead and change all of my information from my previous name Michelle Molsen to Michelle Price. Doing all of this was very exhausting and going to these places cost money for gas, and money to change your license, which also cost money to have your name, changed. Edward did not help me do any of this, and really did not care if I did it or not from the way, he acted. After getting all my information legal, I changed my name on face-book and several other social networks I was on.

A few days later Edward received many comments from his friends saying to him "this was a terrible way of finding out that he had gotten married." When I asked him about this, it made him angry. All I did was asked him why did he not tell any of his friends that he was getting married? So, once again in my life, I totally felt as if someone else was ashamed of me. After asking him these things he told me it was nobody's business and when I told him it made me feel like he was ashamed of marrying me, he then replied all I wanted to do is start drama, and all these things were in my head and I was wrong. Edward was very dominant and liked to turn things to make you think you were the one wrong, but after the time of his telling this girl that was married and when she called on Christmas Eve and him telling her he was alone when I was laying right next to him hurt me. When was he even going to try to understand? So, yes I was feeling, as he did not want anyone to know that he had married me.

Even his closest friend Fred that he had stayed with for years did not know we had gotten married. Fred found out by going out in town and someone telling him. When Fred would call, Edward would not talk to him while I was around. Edward either called him when he was at work or if Edward was home Edward would go outside so I would not know what they talked about. So, I was once again feeling rejection, unwanted and for the life of me, I could not understand why he would do this when we had just gotten married. When Edward and I moved into the double wide mobile home he rented out his single wide home to another one of his friends Russell and his girlfriend of over twelve years and her name was Anita and they had a daughter also and her name was Brittany. Edward only charged them three hundred dollars a month to stay there at his single wide and I was paying way more than three hundred dollars at our home to him for me to stay there with him. When I would bring that up and told Edward that Russell treated his girlfriend Anita way better than Edward treated me, it would make him angry. He said I could not stay with him for free, even though we were married. Then he suggested that maybe since I never had any money at the end of the month, I should get a part time job so I could have some money. Edward knew I could not go to work because I was on disability. I also knew he had many thousands of dollars in the bank and would never help me with any of my bills nor would he put me on his insurance in case I got sick and had to go to the Doctor. I would be stuck paying twenty percent because all disability would pay was eighty percent. I had to go to the Doctor often because of my MS but he did not care. I asked him to put me on his insurance and he said NO because then the company he worked for would take money out of his check. He said he would not allow that because it would make his check smaller every week. So, he would not help me what so ever or help me with any of my medical expenses. When the bills came in, he knew I could not pay them and he would not offer to pay them for me. Edward said that is my responsibility.

When he said that, it made me have all sort of resentment because he had stayed with me for over fourteen months and never did I ask him to pay any of my bills. He didn't even offer to help while staying with me. He was just saving all of his money while staying with me and that was how he was able to buy the double wide we lived in. Edward refused put the house in both of our names. When I asked why he did not put the house in both of our names he would get angry and tell me that I was trying take everything from him. I had never taken anything from him. I could not figure out why he would even suggest that I would try.

Especially with me fixing everything at the house, we were supposed to share. I tried my best to make the house into a doll house and worked my butt off to make this home comfortable. But these things did not matter to Edward; he did not care how much I had done for the house that was supposed to be our home.

Neither Edward nor I went to church, nor were we saved. Edward did not even believe in God, so both of us smoked marijuana and he drank alcohol. I did not drink alcohol except for a few times in my life, but as time progressed with Edward, I found myself drinking like he did.

We were married for just two weeks at this time, and we were already having problems, and I was regretting my decision and I am almost sure he was as well because we had not even made love at this point, and it had been over two weeks. We had ran out of marijuana and Edward had to go to Deep Run which was about a twenty-five minute drive from our home to go and get some more. Edward had been gone for over three hours, I tried calling him over and over on his cell phone, and he never answered. I was getting very worried because he was not answering his phone, because of him driving my car, which was a red Monte Carlo SS, and it stood out and Edward had a habit of driving fast. I did not know if the police or what had stopped him.

I hated the fact he would drive my car because of the gas he used he would never replace and he knew I did not have money to replace what he drove on. So, I had to stay home most of the time unless Tammy Ann would come and get me and we would have lunch once in awhile. Most of the time, she had to pay for that as well, because she knew I had no money. Tammy Ann did not like how Edward was treating me and she was seeing a difference in me since being married to Edward in just this short time.

Edward walked in the back door and he had a few groceries and of course, he had a huge amount of beer, it was the weekend and Edward wanted to make sure he had plenty of beer like he usually did. While he was putting the beer into the refrigerator I noticed his wedding ring was off of his finger. The first thing I asked him was why did he not answer the telephone while I was calling him. Edward's response was he did not want to answer the phone while he was at his friend's house that he got the marijuana from would make him nervous if he answered the phone, as he was saying this to me I knew that was not correct, then I asked him why did it take him so long? Then Edward said why are you asking me so many questions. I said because Edward I noticed you have taken off your wedding ring. When I said that he was like a deer caught in headlights, he did not know what to say but when he did answer my question, he said it was because he needed to "air out his finger."

When Edward said that he seen the look on my face and he knew I knew he was lying, and that excuse was a very poor excuse. When he saw my face, he had seen my eyes fill with water from hurt because he had promised me he would never do that to me, and he did. After he did that, it made me wonder how many other times has he done that, but he just did not get caught. I had already had such insecurity's in my life due to so many others that have abused me during my life including my own family. To me it seemed that my family cared more about Edward than they did me, the whole time fixing up this double wide home for Edward and myself I often asked my Mother to come to see what I had done. Not one time did my Mother come and my Father only came once. I felt like no matter who I was with, I just never mattered to anyone including Edward and my family.

All my life the only people that I had that really cared about me was Tammy Ann and her husband Brent, and my precious children Justin, Jordan and my baby Meghan. When I called Tammy Ann to tell her about the ring that had been removed off of Edward's finger, she could not believe it and told me that this marriage was a big mistake. Then she said, "Michelle the day your were suppose to get married you were so sick that you could not get married that day, and you had to wait till the next day." She continued by saying, "Michelle I believe that was a sign from God." As Tammy Ann was telling me all of this, I knew what she was saying made sense. I have always believed in God but because of all the bad things that have happened in my life, I had such problems with the faith part of being saved and serving God the way I should.

When Edward knew he had hurt me so badly, he said to me I was making more out of this than I should. However, to me it did not seem to me that he cared about what he had done. Edward was the type that never said he was sorry for anything even though he knew he was totally wrong. When I was wrong about things I had to beg for his forgiveness and when we would get into a disagreement Edward would always bring up my past. He would always make everything my fault and he never had any faults or would he even admit to any.

After him hurting me so badly, I slept on the couch for several nights and when he was gone during the day I would stand at the window at the kitchen sink and would just cry, praying to God even though I did not go to church to make my life better, and asking God to make Edward love me. I wanted a better life, and just was not sure how to get what I wanted. I tried so hard to show Edward my love but he never tried to show me his love towards me. When Edward would come home, from work I always had dinner made and I waited on him hand and foot. I always laid his clothes out for the next day, the laundry was always done, and the house was always clean. To Edward that was not enough, he still wanted me to go and get a job, and that is all he would talk about. Still after being now over three weeks to this point we still have not even made love since being married or even showed love towards each other. When Edward would come in all he would do when he walked in the back door is first take off his shoes, then get a beer our of the refrigerator and then sit on the computer and play his games. Edward would not even hug or kiss me when he came home or show me any kind of affection, and especially on Monday's he would not even want to talk to me.

I tried talking to Edward of why he had not even made love to me since we got married. When I asked him about this he said, "Michelle it is Monday and I really do not want to talk about anything. I am tired and all you do is sit here and think of things to get mad about." I could not believe that because that was so untrue all I wanted to know why he was acting like he was. I just could not understand that we have almost been married for three weeks and we still have not even made love once since being married and his behavior had changed so much since getting married. Finally, after him seeing me cry he said why would I want to make love to you when all you do is try and find something wrong all the time. I then said Edward you have hurt me terribly bad by taking off your ring. You have not told anyone that you know we even got married. I am hurt, and you have hurt me, and you have not once said you are sorry and you never say you're sorry for how you act about anything. All you do is push your wrongs or your behavior under the rug and never want to talk about real issues between us.

Then I said all you want to talk about is things that are wrong on your job and hear all your complaints about this one and another one, as if I know anything about your electrical work or even the people you are talking about. I then said Edward I love you and I want to spend the rest of my life with you but you act and have showed me you do not even want anyone to even know you are married and you have not even made love to me since being married. When I continued on trying to talk to him, he hit his fist on the desk where the computer was and told he had enough of me talking. Then he said the reason he did not want any one at his job to know he was married was because it was no one's business that he had gotten married. When Edward said that it even hurt me even more because once again I felt shame, and I was not worth being bragged about by being married to Edward, so once again I slept on the couch another night. While laying on the couch that night I could not figure out why Edward was always so tired on Monday's when he worked ten hour days Monday thru Thursday and always off on Friday, Saturday and Sunday's. So, to me he got plenty of rest because he only worked four days a week and he was off three days a week. While Edward was home on his three days he did not have to do anything, I had the yard mowed, the home clean, and all the laundry done and cooked all during the week. On the days he was home I got up every morning, made him breakfast, and cooked for him at night as well. Edward did nothing during these three days except drink his beer, smoke his marijuana, and play his games on the computer. He never took me any where knowing all I did was stay home during the time he was at work. He never helped me clean the kitchen up after cooking for him, nor did he ever help me with any clothes being washed or dried or being folded, or even being put up. Edward never wanted for nothing, I did it all at our home. When I tried, explaining this to him it would make him very angry and said I had way too much time on my hands and once again, he told me I needed to get a job. That to me is all Edward wanted me to do, so since him saying this so often, I eventually got a job. This job was in another restaurant in our local town, when he knew this was very hard for me since having a grill of my own, and having to let it go due to finances and how the economy was at that time however I let my pride down to do this for Edward. Once again, I was getting up at two in the morning to go to this place and make biscuits again and to prepare breakfast for so many that knew me and knew that I had to close my own restaurant.

While going to work at this place, I was insulted so badly by so many. When I told Edward, he actually told me to suck it up, but when it came to his job, I had to listen, and if I did not listen, he would get mad. So when I got the job Edward finally made love to me, and to me that hurt me so badly because I felt like that was the only reason why he did make love to me. I worked at this place for just three weeks, I did not want to do this, nor did I feel like I should just for Edward. I did not like getting up that early in the morning nor did I like having to work on weekends. Standing on my feet would hurt my legs so much because of my MS. When I told Edward I quit, he got very mad at me again, and told me I was going to do what ever I wanted to do and not listen to him. When Edward said that to me I then replied right back and said Edward you do what you want to do as well without corresponding with me about any of your choices, but I am suppose to do what all you want me to do for you.

Of course, after this, another disagreement started and once again, I was on the couch. A week went by and I was still on the couch. It seemed like it did not matter to Edward, and when I went on his face-book page that he left open a girl that he went to school with many years ago wanted to come and see him and this was one of the girls that had gotten mad that she had found out he gotten married. This girl's name was Nadine and she was also married, she had left him an in box note saying she was coming to town and wanted to see him. When she called on Edward's cell phone I answered the phone and was really nice and told her Edward was not home right now however she could come and wait for him until he got home, she then said she would call him later. I then said OK I would give him the message. Nadine was not very nice to me on the phone and acted as if I have done something towards her, and I did not even know this girl except what Edward had told me about her. Edward was a good friend with her brother but her brother had gotten killed in a car accident.

So, when Edward finally got home I told him that Nadine called and wanted to come by the house, and then I told him I told her she could come to our home to wait on him. I also told Edward how she had spoken to me on the phone and when I told him this, he rolled his eyes at me, as if I was making it all up. Edward had just gotten home from the grocery store but he made the excuse he had forgotten something and he left again but this time he took his phone. Edward was gone for over two hours and I knew what was going on and when he got home from going to the grocery store I asked him if he met Nadine some where he said No but I knew different because of how he was acting. I then thought to myself just how many married women did he know and just how many married women did he have affairs with, because all of this was not adding up for me. So again we were having another argument once again and of course this was all in my head from what Edward was saying. When I called Tammy Ann about all of this she too was thinking the very same thing I was thinking that he met her. Tammy Ann knew just how badly I had been hurt just in the few short weeks of being married.

Chapter 15 More Medical Problems and Bad Habits

A couple months after being married to Edward, I found a knot in my left breast. About nine years prior to knowing Edward, I had to have surgery on both breasts, and since then I had to have MRI's and Mammograms every six months to make sure I had no more knots to come up. When I found this knot on my left breast, I immediately made an appointment to get the tests done again. Sure enough, this knot had to be removed and when I told Edward about this, he acted as if it was no big deal. I was told that this knot had to be removed and that they needed to send the knot off to a pathologist to make sure it was not breast cancer. So while I was there at the Doctor I asked them how much would I need to have to pay for this? Being on disability and knowing disability only paid eighty percent. When they told me, I knew I was about two hundred and ninety dollars short, so when Edward came home from work I told him what I needed him to help me do. Edward agreed to help me but he stated to me that when I got paid next month from my disability check I needed to pay him back. That hurt me so badly because Edward had a lot of money in the bank and he knew I struggled to just pay my monthly bills. However, Edward did not even care about my financial situation what so ever.

When the day came for my surgery instead of my husband going with me, my best friend Tammy Ann had to take me. Edward did not want to even take that day off from work to go with me even though he knew I was really scared about the outcome. Edward did not even offer Tammy Ann any gas money for her taking me when Edward knew I was absolutely broke. Edward did not even thank Tammy Ann for taking me so he could go to work. When the surgery finally got over with and they told us everything, looked fine Tammy Ann tried calling Edward but he did not even answer his phone. This made Tammy Ann so mad, and for the life of her, she could not understand why he would not even take me to begin with. But, what really made her mad was Edward acted as if he really did not care about the results or about my well being or my health.

Tammy Ann stated to me that she treated her dog, better than Edward treated me, and deep down I knew she was right but once again in my life I felt as if I did not deserve any better than what I was getting. I talked to Tammy Ann about everything she was my very best friend, and she knew I was changing little by little to the point I did not even believe in myself any longer, and that Edward was the cause of this changing. Tammy Ann could not understand why Edward would never give me any money at all, and when I fell short at the end of the month, I would always have to call Tammy Ann to help me to get through till the end of the month. When I told Tammy Ann about the two hundred and ninety dollars this did make her very angry and she said "Michelle I would not pay him nothing" then she was telling me that is what a husband is suppose to do, and that is to take care of you. Then Tammy Ann said that her husband Brent would never treat her, the way Edward was treating me. I told Tammy Ann that I had to pay him back or it would be another great big argument, and I was so tired of talking to Edward about money and arguing about money all the time. When I told her this, she just shook her head and when she did that, I knew she was feeling so badly for me.

When Edward finally got home from working at Camp Lejuene in Jacksonville, NC which was about a forty minute drive from our home, he walked in and the first thing he did was take off his work boots. I was lying on the couch in the living room, resting from the surgery. He then went straight to the fridge to get a beer and get on the computer. He did not even ask me how I was feeling or what the Doctor said. I finally asked him if he wanted to know what the Doctor said. Edward turned the computer chair towards me and said yeah, and just had this look on his face as if he really did not care. When I told him that everything was good and I just had to keep going back every six months for my breast exams, so they could continue checking them. Edward did not say that was great news, he did not ask how I was feeling, he just turned the computer chair back and started once again playing his computer games.

When I saw he did not even want to talk to me about any of this, I just turned my head and started watching television. I wasn't really watching the television. I was just thinking about his reactions and while I thought about how he really did not care what I had been through that day, tears just filled my eyes once again. This seemed to happen so many times since being married to Edward in just the few months we were married. After all that which had happened, he asked me what were we going to eat for dinner. I said Edward

I had just had surgery and I did not cook dinner that I did not feel like cooking dinner. Edward got upset and said so what does that mean? I said Edward you can go out and get us something to eat. He then said, "Michelle I have worked all day and I am tired and do not feel like going anywhere." The real problem was he had already drunk some beers. That was the real reason why he did not want to go and get us something to eat. So, after just having surgery and lying on the couch, I had to get up and make us something to eat for dinner. While I was in the kitchen making dinner for the both of us, he stayed on the computer playing his games instead of getting up to help me. He did not help me clean the kitchen up after dinner either. Edward was the type that he did not eat dinner until really late because he made sure he had drank enough beer to get drunk first before eating dinner. He also knew I would not go to bed until the kitchen was clean. Edward would not eat dinner until it was past nine o'clock at night and sometimes much later.

This really bothered me and made me feel as if that is all he married me for, just to take care of him but he did not take care of me. To save money I did not want to go back to my breast Doctor to get the stitches out, I took them out myself. When I got my disability check on the third of the next month Edward asked me if I had gone to the bank to get his two hundred and ninety dollars back. I said yes, in hopes, he would not take the money but he did. Once again, I was so hurt that I felt he loved money way more than he loved me. So often when I was broke and he knew I was broke, he would just tell me to get a job. Edward did not care about my health issues even though before we got married he knew I had many health issues and he would not help me by putting me on his insurance, which he knew that if he would do this it would help me so much. If he had put me on his insurance that would allow me to go to the Doctor without having to pay the Doctor anything, and I would be able to take care of all of my health issues.

So often I had to call my boys Justin and Jordan to just loan me some money to help me to just buy my prescriptions that I needed every month because Edward would not buy them for me knowing I needed them because of my MS. I hated calling Tammy Ann, and my children Justin and Jordan to loan me money to help me buy medication. Each time that I had to do it, which was often I would have to hear from each of them how bad Edward was and that he should have been the one that should help me buy my medications. I knew they were right but I had to have my medicine so they would loan me the money.

So. Often after Tammy Ann and my children would fuss at me about borrowing money from them for helping me buy the medication that I needed, I would go months without my medication. My body would hurt so badly and I would be in a lot of pain and aches from the MS. When I would go to bed my muscles would have so many muscle jerks in my legs, my arms and even my hands would fold up in such a way that I could not even straighten out my fingers which hurt so badly and would wake me up when I was asleep. Sometimes this even happened during the day because my body needed my MS medicine. One time I woke Edward up to help me. I just needed him to help me rub the aches out of my legs. When I asked him he cursed me out, and told me he had to work the next day, while I would be sitting at home doing nothing. This hurt my feelings so badly, and I cried myself to sleep from the pain.

Sometimes, I would even run a bath tub full of hot water to help my muscles so they would relax. Edward would even get mad about that because he said I was keeping him from sleeping with the noise. While I was in the bath tub trying to get my muscles to relax, I kept thinking about how when he would come home and he would tell me how his joints would hurt so badly. He said he had arthritis in his hands, and when he would hurt I would rub them so he would feel better but once again when it came to me he did not help me in any way even little simple things as that. I was beginning to see things so clearly as if I was having a relationship just like my Mother and Father.

I was starting to understand why my Father drank alcohol and became an alcoholic for so many years and especially when I was a child. Thinking about all of this I was beginning to understand why I was drinking, it was the same reason why my Father did, he lived with someone and was married to the same kind of person I was. A person that was all about themselves, never happy, they never smiled, never joked, and always had a very dry sense of humor. The only thing that made both my Mother and my husband Edward happy was monetary items or things. It was all about money with both of them, and neither one of them were ever happy about anything except when it came to money or what they could have.

I never saw my Mother happy about anything and she would hardly ever smile in her life, the same as Edward he would never smile about anything neither. I was beginning to fall short on my promise of never drinking or becoming an alcoholic like my Father did. I was finding myself drinking just like my Father did in his own life, and before I knew it I was becoming an alcoholic just like my Father and Edward.

Eventually I found myself starting to drink beer and then I started smoking marijuana. I found myself doing this everyday, the taste of beer was something I got use to very quickly, and it was becoming a very bad habit. I would start drinking first thing in the morning. Then not only was I starting to drink every single day and smoke marijuana every day but I also got put on nerve pills xanax, and that combination was helping me cope with all of Edward's behavior and how he treated me. I was being hurt so bad from Edward that I was just trying to find anything to help me deal with all my terrible thoughts of the past, and the thoughts I was having of always feeling so unloved and not wanted by anyone except by Tammy Ann and my children.

When my children would come to visit, they started noticing that every time they saw me I was holding a beer can, and they knew that was not me at all. At first, they did not say anything, and this was something I did not talk to Tammy Ann about because I was in fear if she knew I would lose her friendship. Eventually I started finding myself withdrawing from all of my friends, and especially Tammy Ann when I was drinking or smoking marijuana because I did not want anyone to know what was going on with me. So, I would just always stay at home, I was becoming a loner, and not wanting to talk to anyone, several times Tammy Ann would call and ask me if I wanted to go to lunch or some shopping. I would always say no and lie and say I was not feeling good, or make up some other reason.

Edward was finally beating me down so badly that the only way I could feel better about who I was, was to do what he was doing. I found myself becoming a full blown alcoholic just like Edward and my father. This was something I promised myself as a child I would never do. However, after starting doing this I found that mine and Edward's relationship was improving, he liked the fact that I was not hanging out with Tammy Ann much anymore. He also like that my children did not visit me like they used to do. I was becoming what he wanted. A wife that stayed at home and someone that was just as screwed up as he was.

When I did this, we started talking but never about real issues and if he did hurt my feelings it helped that I was drinking the alcohol because I did not feel the pain like I used to feel when I did not drink or do drugs. One day to my surprise, my boys Justin and Jordan came to our home when Edward was at work, and when they walked in they could tell I had been drinking and it was early in the morning. Justin said "Momma do you remember when you got sick with MS in 2001? " I said, "yes, Justin why are you bringing that up?" He then said, "Momma do you remember when you started drinking Crown Royal for two weeks when you found out you were sick with MS?" I said, "Yes Justin." Then Justin said, "Momma do you remember when Jordan and I put ex-lax in your drink and you drunk it and it made you sick for two days?" I started laughing but neither Justin nor Jordan laughed. They told me that they did not like seeing me like this and that I was becoming an alcoholic. When they said that to me, I replied like all alcoholics do to their families. I told them I was not an alcoholic. I hid how much I was drinking from my boys because I knew I was headed down the path of self destruction. I told the boys that I would slow down but I did not slow down.

I began drinking even more. All of my past, all of my current pain, was the reason I was drinking, and how Edward treated me was another reason. It seemed like as long as I was drinking the more Edward and I got along. I knew my children did not like this and the habit of drinking alcohol and because of that, it seemed that they stopped visiting me as much or called me as they usually did. This was something Edward liked very much because Edward did not like my children at all, and would often call them very bad words and also say bad things about my daughter Meghan as well. Not only that Edward would often throw up in my face how I had four children and all four of my children being conceived by different men and was calling me ugly words as well.

So drinking the alcohol was something that would take the hurt away, the pain away, and was something I could use to ignore all of his comments about myself and my children. One time Edward even accused me of being intimate with my son Jordan because Jordan and I had a real close bond and Edward was really jealous of that bond. When Edward said that to me it crushed me and once again I had someone telling me I was a horrible Mother just like my own Mother said I was, however Edward would never talk about his own Mother whom had been married way more than me and married one alcoholic right after another one. Edward knew the right buttons to push with me because he knew all of my past and how I lost Angel to my parents. I loved my children and would do anything for each of them. The bond Jordan and I had was because we both loved sports and when ever he needed my help I was always there for him, just as I was to the other children as well. Edward knew what to say to hurt me and make me feel as if I was nothing just like my own Mother would make me feel all of my life.

When Edward said that to me about my son Jordan is because Edward hated him the most and it seemed like the only conversation we would ever have was always about Jordan. My son Jordan's initials were J.A.M. and when I would talk about Jordan Edward would talk so cruelly about my son. One time Edward called Jordan by his initials and I asked him what he meant by that. Edward replied that his initials meant "Just Another Mistake." I could not understand why he hated Jordan so much because if you really got to know Jordan you would find that he was a very good boy. He had always been a Momma's boy, but not because of what Edward had excused me of.

When he excused me of that it blew my mind because Edward knew me and knew what kind of Mother I was. He knew that I would never hurt my children in any kind of way; my children were all I had all during my adult life. They were not only my children but they had each become my best friends. Each of them knew that could talk about anything with me. I, in return, talked to them about things in my life. We were always that way and Edward was so jealous that my children and I were so close in everything and in every way. My children would tell me the good, the bad, and the ugly no matter what.

We always had a motto and that said, "We were strong, we were tough, and we always stick together. According to Edward he said that was something, only black people would say. Edward was a racist and he could not understand why I had not raised my children to be that way, Edward would use the "N" word continuously. He was always accusing Jordan of wanting to be one, because he had always had black friends, and I never had a problem with that.

I did not like Edward saying them kind of things about the black race and thought how ignorant he was for saying and acting like that towards the black race. Edward and I got into a great big argument about what he had said about Jordan and me. Of course, I could not get a word in, so the following day while he was at work I wrote Edward a three page letter trying to explain to him why my children and I were so close I put this letter on his dresser so when he got home he would see it and read it. That letter stayed on his dresser for three months and not one time did he ever read one word of that letter.

I eventually threw the letter in the trash because I knew Edward could care less about anything I felt much less what I said in that letter. When I brought up the subject about the letter that he did not read he told me all he wanted to do is to tie Jordan to a tree and beat him to a pulp, and make him bleed to death. When Edward said that he made me cry, because for the life of me I could not understand why Edward had so much anger towards my children.

Edward also put down my son Justin who was in the Navy and had already served a term in Afghanistan. Instead of Edward being thankful that Justin had served our country, he would call him a girl and talked about him in not nice terms. He accused Justin of being a wimp. But Edward had never served in the Military. And I am sure he could of not of done anything in his own life that Justin had already done in his tender years of life of just being twenty years of age. Justin had already accomplished more at twenty than Edward had done at forty five years of age. I am very proud of my children and I could not understand why Edward could not see just how wonderful they were and still are. Listening to all of this from Edward made me feel more and more hatred towards Edward, and would cause me to drink more, and to take more xanax just to cope with him. When Edward would go out of town for the four days of him working and he would have to stay in a hotel because he was working too far from home, that he would decide to stay in a hotel instead of coming home. Those days were the only days that I did not feel as if I was walking on egg shells.

Chapter 16 Getting Sick of Tired of being Sick and Tired

One occasion I had bought some sod grass for our front yard because it was just sand. My brother Joe told me about this man that had done a great job in his yard so I hired this man to bring us some sod. It was another rainy day and cold and this contractor brought me eight pallets of sod to go into the front yard, and it was centipede grass, which I might add was very expensive. I thought this would be a great present for Edward and make him very happy. The day the sod came I went out and lifted the heavy square sods of grass from each pallet to put grass onto the front yard, the only problem was you had to keep it watered so it would take root in the sand. I worked all day and was very tired but so proud of how the yard looked. It finally had grass. I was waited so patiently, for Edward to come home and see what a great job I had done and on top of it, I had paid for all of it which cost me over twelve hundred dollars.

About six thirty that evening, his work van came up the driveway. As soon as he walked into the house, he started cursing at me. He informed me that it was laid improperly. He was furious that he had worked all day and now he had to go out and fix this "N" mess. Immediately my feelings were hurt. I had tried to do something good for him and all I had received was the sharp side of his tongue. I was told I had done a horrible job laying the grass.

So, as Edward grabbed a beer, and went outside to fix the mess he said I had made. I stayed in the kitchen feeling useless and under appreciated. After crying, I went out and helped him move the grass to where he wanted it. To me no matter what I tried to do to make this man happy it just never seemed like I could. He would just fuss and complain just like my Mother had. Never was anything good enough even if he did not have to pay for any of it.

I had saved for months to get this done for Edward, but it was not appreciated in any kind of way. Edward never apologized for anything, of how he acted, or the words he would say to me, nothing was ever were right according to Edward. It just seemed like I never satisfied Edward in any way, no matter how hard I tried. Edward would curse me out and I would cry. I would cry so hard that my MS would act up. Then I would stutter because of my MS. Then he would then make fun of how I talked which made me feel even worse. I already had self esteem issues from the many medical problems I had, but that never seemed to matter to Edward. He would just make fun of me and hurt my feelings even more.

Edward would love on our cat named key. Sometimes he would love on our dog Molly, but he would also whip Molly every day telling her, he was sure; she had done something wrong and deserved to be whipped.

When I asked Edward for anything, simple like a pack of cigarettes he would make me pay him back. So many times Edward would go out of town and stay gone for four days, and when he left he knew there were hardly any groceries in the house and he knew I had no money to get any, and when he was gone he would eat breakfast, lunch and dinner. When he would call the house to make sure I was there I would ask him what he ate for lunch and would tell me what a terrific lunch he would had. He knew I was at home with nothing more than a soup or a sandwich. This did not even make him feel bad, and while we were on the phone with each other most of the time it was just silence, we had noting to say to one another. If we did talk it, was either how bad my children were or about his job that I knew nothing about or wanted to know nothing about, in other words the whole conversation was completely boring.

The only person that was even concerned about me eating was my best friend Tammy Ann. She would take me to lunch several times during the week just to make sure I at least ate one good meal a day. Edward never left me any money for food or anything that I might need while he was gone. Tammy Ann said to me on several occasions that I acted completely different when Edward was gone. I knew this but I did not say much because I knew why, but I knew if I told Tammy Ann the real reason why I acted different, this would only make Tammy Ann not like Edward even more. However, Tammy Ann was not stupid she already knew the reason why I acted so much different; it was because my nerves were not torn up, while Edward was gone. When Edward was home my nerves were always torn up, and I always walked on egg shells when he was home. When my children would come to our home, the way Edward acted almost made me sick to my stomach. Edward made my children feel so unwelcome when they only would come to see their Mother. My children and I would just stay in the kitchen, while he was on the computer in the living room while they were there. As soon as my children left, they never said bye to Edward but they always hugged me and said Momma we love you. I hated seeing my children leave because I knew as soon as my children left Edward would always have something negative to say about each one of them and especially Jordan.

Edward could not say a sentence without using a curse word in the sentence. It had always been like that. When I would talk to him about cursing at home, I would tell him that I was his wife and he should show me more respect than that. He said that is how he talked on his job, I then said well Edward leave it on your job, but do not bring that language home. Then he said this was his house and he would talk how he wanted too. Edward had no feelings what so ever and he showed that.

So, one day while he was at work I thought of something that would tell me if he felt something or not. When Edward came home of course he would do the same thing as Edward did every single day, he would grab a beer and go straight to the computer, so while he was sitting on the computer chair, I went up next to him and I pinched him under his upper forearm as hard as I could. Edward jumped up and said what did you do that for? I said Edward I just wanted to know if you felt anything. When I said that of course, I got cursed out and was told not to ever do that again, but at least then I knew he did feel pain but he never expressed it as I did. The next day he had a tremendous bruise under his upper arm where I had pinched him to see if he had any feelings any at all. I was wiling to do anything to see if Edward had any feelings, because he never acted as if he had any feelings.

Eventually trying so hard to do everything within my power to please Edward I was getting sick and tired of being sick and tired. I was beginning to lose everything good in my life. One by one, my children were moving to Georgia to be close to the Meghan's family. This was exactly what Edward wanted; he wanted all my children gone and my best friend as well. Edward did not want me to have anyone, and that was his plans all along, he did not want me to have anyone except for him, which would make my life completely miserable. Edward was a type of person that he did not require friends. Nor did he have any, and he expected my life to be the same he was making everyone in my life that I loved so much disappear.

When I sold my house that was next to my best friend Tammy Ann, she told me this from the very beginning. I told Tammy Ann that I loved Edward with all my heart and I did not feel that what Edward said to me when he said to me he loved me I felt that was not true. Tammy Ann also told me that Edward should be a better person to me, and all I could say is Tammy Ann I think I could teach Edward how to love. When I said that Tammy Ann said to me you can not teach someone to love that is something that should come easy, something you should not have to work for as hard as you work for love from Edward, Michelle. Then Tammy Ann said to me, he should take care of you and make sure you have food to eat while he is gone out of town while he is at work, and he does not, then she said Michelle don't you think you deserve way more than what you are getting? When Tammy Ann would say those things to me, I knew she was right and I wanted to be treated different but I was not sure I deserved any better.

So all I did was just stay and put up with all the abusive language, abusive behavior, and then it began to get physical from Edward. Sometimes when Edward would get abusive towards me and make it so hard that all I would do is cry so much that when he did this from his drinking. I would pack up a few clothes and camp out at a lake close to our home. I would have no money, or anything to eat so Edward would know I would eventually be back, and he was right. Sadly, enough this was all true but I stayed and camped out as long as I could. I knew I would only have to listen to Edward just a few hours of cursing and fighting because I knew he had to go to bed to go to work on Monday.

When I did this it never taught Edward a lesson all it did was tell him I would always come back and that is just what he wanted to know, so he knew he could treat me any way he wanted to treat me. So I learned that I had to take it, and just live with it because I made a very poor decision, I should have never sold my house just like Tammy Ann had told me many times. Tammy Ann saw things from the outside. I was so in love with Edward that I did not see his intentions or what he was planning. It finally got to the place I was not mad at Edward. I was truly mad with myself.

I thought I was smarter than this from so many poor decisions from my past but the love I had for Edward blinded me in a way I have never ever in my life been so blinded by my love for him. It got so bad that when I would talk to Tammy Ann all we had to talk about was Edward; she eventually got so sick of it she told me that she had enough of talking about all the bad about Edward when I did nothing about it. Tammy Ann said to me that I had to come to a decision either our friendship or Edward, and she was serious. Tammy Ann told me she was so sick and tired of seeing me being mentally and emotionally abused by Edward. Tammy Ann could not stand Edward, so many times she saw how Edward treated me but she knew just how much I loved him, I would cry when she would tell me this, and said to me Michelle just cry do what ever you have to do but get out of this marriage it is NOT no good for you.

Tammy Ann was right because after all of this I began to drink more and more that when I would wake up in the morning the first thing I wanted was to just drink beer. But, it was no fun to drink alone, so I called the girl that lived in Edward's rented single wide mobile home, and we would drink almost all morning long. It finally got to the point that I did not go anywhere, I would just stay home and drink, cry, and pace back and forth, my nerves were completely torn up from Edward. It got so bad that when her boyfriend was at work and Edward was at work we would actually count pennies just to drink more beer, then we would walk in the woods to throw the beer cans away so no one would know especially her boyfriend and Edward. I would always make sure Edward would have the same amount of beer in the refrigerator when he left for work that the same amount would be there when he got home from work, because it got to the point he was counting his beers before leaving in the morning to go to work.

When I first got with Edward I looked great, acted great, friendly, and so many people knew me, but after marrying Edward that when I looked in the mirror I seen a complete different person. A person that had changed so much, a person that was so sad, just wanting him to love me so desperately. I was a person that laughed, and smiled, and was happy since marrying Edward my life changed so much that when I looked in the mirror I saw a sad person. A person that cried most everyday, a person that never left the house, a person that never put make up on or even did my hair, I was beginning to be my Mother. I was a sad and miserable person. Little by little Tammy Ann was noticing all of it, she asked me why did not wear girl clothes anymore, I did not want to tell her why, but I knew why. I did not feel attractive, nor was I happy. The whole time being with Edward he only said three things that were good about me and those things were, I was a good cook, a good painter, and a good house keeper. When Edward said them things to me that hurt me so badly, he never gave me any compliments any of all.

A few weeks later my Father called and asked me if Edward would come and put up some flood lights since Edward was an electrician, of course the same as Edward I tried as hard to please my parents as I did Edward. So, I immediately asked Edward to go to my parents to put up flood lights for my Father. Edward did not really want to do this, but he at least he did that. Once we got to my parents we all were sitting in the living room, and as we all were talking and all of a sudden, my Father said to Edward that he felt sorry for him that he married me. Then my Father said to Edward he was going to send Edward a sympathy card for marrying me, when my Father said that, it took all I could do is keep my eyes from dropping tears, because I did not want anyone seeing me cry, because that would make both Edward and my Father completely happy. When my Father said that ugly comment even my Mother laughed, they loved Edward and thought he was great, but they had no idea how he treated their daughter.

As my Father and Edward went outside to where my Father wanted the flood lights at he left Edward outside alone. When my Father came back in the house, he said to me that if I messed this marriage up, he would whip my tail, but when my Father said that, he did not say it such nice words as that. I wondered if he would think so highly of Edward if he only knew how he treated his daughter, as always I never told my parents anything about my life except about the grill that my sister and Mother ruined that business for me. Every marriage I had I never told my parents what was done to me, even when I was in a coma, and had a hot curling iron was stuck inside of me because I refused to have sexual relationship with my very first husband. It was because of all of this I lost my first daughter Angel to my Mother.

I had so much running through my head, why would my Father think Edward was so special and never say anything to me that was good. I was so used to being put down, and feeling as I was not worthy of nothing that was good. When Edward finally got their flood lights up, I was so ready to leave my parent's house. I hated being there because the whole time, I felt no love at all from my parents. When my Father said that to Edward that treated me so badly was, like as if my own Father spit in my face as if he was completely ashamed of me. Finally, we left and on the way home I stared out the window so Edward could not see my face, tears just flowed down my face. I kept wondering why my parents did not love me and why my own Father would say something that was so cruel about me. All that did was give Edward more reasons to put me down because then he knew just how my own parents felt about me, and so many times after that he would throw that up in my face so often.

As soon as we got home this time, I grabbed a beer and I went outside, got my phone, called Tammy Ann, and told her what had happened. I was crying, she knew I was hurt, and being the friend, she was she would just listen and sometimes even cry with me, she felt so bad for me, and this made her so mad. There was nothing she could do when it came to my parents or Edward. The only thing she said to me was, "Michelle, why do you subject yourself to go there and each time when you go you get hurt by something they say to you?" I told her I loved them she asked my why do you love them? I said Tammy Ann they are my parents and I am suppose to love them. After that she did not say anything, more but I completely understood what she was saying.

Chapter 17 Being a Better Mother than what I had

Meghan had already moved to Georgia to live with her Grandparents because she did not want to live with me, but it was not because of me it was because of Edward. Meghan called me and said "Momma I need a car." Well, I was already thinking of getting me a different car because I had a Monte Carlo SS and it sat down low on the ground and it was difficult for me to get in and get out of the car. At the time Meghan had called me and asked me to help her get a car so she could get back and forth to work, Edward was working out of town and I did not feel like I needed his permission to get another car if I was going to be the one that was going to make the payments.

So, while Edward was out of town I went to a local car dealer and bought a Kia Sorrento, it was Burgundy and had plenty of room, and sat high off the ground just like something I was looking for. I could now give my Monte Carlo SS to my daughter Meghan so she could have a car to get back and forth to go to work. When Edward came home and saw what I had done, he was so mad and as usual, I got cursed out. The entire weekend he cursed at me saying such abusive words and hurting me as usual. I tried explaining to him why I did this he did not want to hear one word from me, all he said was you have to pay every cent for it and he was not going to pay one cent for this vehicle or even help me pay for the insurance.

It did not matter to him that my daughter who was only eighteen years old needed her Mother's help. Growing up my children only had me to depend on and that was something they were all three used to. When they needed help, they would call their Mother and I was always there no matter what. It was getting close to Meghan's birthday as well, so I thought that would be a great birthday present as well. I told Edward I was going to take Meghan the Monte Carlo and asked him to help me get it to her. When I asked him to help me to carry this car to Georgia, it was like I asked Edward to cut off his arm.

Edward immediately said no he would not do anything to help me. I called Tammy Ann and asked if she would help me get this car to Meghan. Of course, when I asked Tammy Ann if she would help me get the car to Meghan she agreed to help me the following weekend, so I then called Meghan and told her my plans, this made my daughter so very happy and by her being happy this made me happy as well.

When the weekend approached, I was so excited because Tammy Ann and I were going to spend the entire weekend in Georgia. We also were going to River Street, something Tammy Ann had never seen, and it had been a very long time since I had been there myself. I was so excited about taking this trip, one because I would not be home during the weekend while Edward was home. Two, I was also getting to see my daughter. And, three, I was spending time with my very best friend and going to go to River Street in Georgia.

Tammy Ann got to meet my family in Georgia, and Edward had never met anyone of my family in Georgia nor did he want to. So early Friday morning Tammy Ann and I left she drove the Monte Carlo and I drove my new Kia. We had a six hour drive ahead of us. We finally made it to Georgia, Meghan was so happy to see us both, and her family made us feels very welcomed like they usually did to me. I have known this family for over twenty-three years and even though their son and I divorced we all still remained friends, and they still had my picture and pictures of all my children on their walls.

Tammy Ann and I went out to eat in Metter, Georgia where Meghan's family lived and soon after Meghan and her Grandparents went out and ate with us. Tammy Ann and I had already decided we would not stay with Meghan's grandparents, that we would rent a hotel room right there in Metter, Georgia and Meghan would stay with us because the next day we were planning a trip to go to Savannah, Georgia to go to River Street with Meghan to celebrate her birthday with her.

While we were in Georgia Brent, Tammy Ann's husband called her numerous times to make sure we made it safely and asked us if we were having a good time. When Tammy Ann and I got together, we always had a wonderful time. We would laugh, talk and joke the entire time. We went to one store that we laughed so hard we all about to wet our pants from laughing so much. It did not matter where Tammy Ann and I would go we would always have such a wonderful time, we were the best of best of friends, and we were so much a like in so many ways.

Sometimes though I was jealous of Tammy Ann's marriage because her husband cared so much about her that he called her several times while we were gone but Edward never called me once, he did not even call me to find out if we made it safely. Edward was mad about me buying the car to begin with. When he saw that it was a Kia, he immediately said all I wanted, was to be just like Tammy Ann. She also owned a Kia so for Edward; he did not care if I or Tammy Ann made it safely or not. It was always about Edward; he did not care about me, and my children all he cared about was his money, his job, but mostly himself. I never let on that it hurt me when Edward did not call me because this weekend was supposed to be about Meghan, not my feelings towards Edward.

Since Tammy Ann and I were so close, it was almost like we could read each other's thoughts. We were as close as if we were actual sisters. She knew why I acted sort of depressed. While Meghan was in the shower at the hotel, she said to me Michelle it is Edward's loss and if he actually loved you he would have called you at least. It would not matter if he were mad at you or not. I knew Tammy Ann was right but as soon as Meghan got out of the shower, we stopped talking about that subject, so Meghan would not know something was wrong. We continued getting ready for the great day; we were going to have with Meghan so she could have a wonderful birthday.

Once we got to River Street, Meghan and Tammy Ann were so impressed and we went from store to store and had such a wonderful time. We took pictures, ate outside in some of the nicest places and the weather was so wonderful, and the food was delicious. We would watch people walk by and see all sorts of things that were so funny and we would laugh so hard. Tammy Ann and I knew we would be leaving soon because later that day we were planning on coming back home. Tammy Ann's husband would be home on Sunday and because she did not get to see him that much she wanted to be there when he returned home. I completely understood that because Tammy Ann and Brent's marriage was way different than my marriage with Edward.

Tammy Ann, Meghan, and I went into this store that would be so great for a teenager and Meghan found this dress, it was quite expensive but since I did not get to see her very often I bought the dress for her for her birthday. I also bought Tammy Ann something as a souvenir to always remind her of our wonderful trip in Savannah, Georgia. So, as we were taking Meghan back to Metter, Georgia and were saying our good byes to her and her family, in my heart I was dreading this trip back home.

I knew why Tammy Ann wanted to go back home to go and be with her husband, but my husband was not anything like hers was. The whole nine years of knowing Tammy Ann and Brent I have never known them to even say one ugly word to one another much less Brent curse her and make her feel worthless as Edward did to me. As Tammy Ann and I was heading down the highway and barely got past the Georgia lines to the South Carolina lines were about an hour, about that time my phone finally beeped indicating I had a text. I was sort of excited and hoping it was Edward to just tell me he missed me and he loved me. When I opened my phone, up sure enough it was Edward but his text was something I did not want to see. His text to me said: I hope you have two hundred and seventy dollars because that is how much our water bill is for the grass sod you bought for the yard.

I just could not believe it; I had just had a wonderful day with my very best friend and my daughter Meghan. Edward started texting me over and over, cursing about the water bill. While, Tammy Ann and I were gone, Edward had received the water bill. But, because I had purchased the sod, Edward felt like I should pay for the water bill as well. I just could not understand why he would say I had to pay the entire water bill because he was the one that was watering the brand new sod that I had paid for. I had already told Edward that the grass did not need to be watered every single day. I told him that it only needed to be watered every other day. Edward never listened to anything I had to say. He always did what he wanted to do, but the entire six hour drive my phone kept getting text after text about the water bill.

I knew for a fact that he had thousands of dollars in the bank and he knew I had no money because of my disability. He was just angry because I bought a new car. He knew that I would have a car payment as well. I could not understand why he was so upset about me giving the car to Meghan because he even complained about getting in and out of the Monte Carlo. I actually thought I was doing something good but because I did not ask him he over reacted. In one of the text message he brought up the Kia and he called it "Killed In Action."

This six hour drive seemed to be the longest drive of my life getting negative text after negative text from Edward. Eventually I started once again crying telling Tammy Ann I did not even want to go home. Tammy Ann said to me she could hardly blame me and that Edward was doing this just to hurt me. That is when I finally admitted to Tammy Ann that I felt like I had made a huge mistake by marrying Edward. I knew that he did not love me nor had he loved me since being married. He just loved everything I did for house he had purchased and the things I had done for him during the time I sold my grill and my home while I had some money. Tammy Ann told me that when I got home to just go to bed and try to ignore his nasty comments. As I dropped Tammy Ann off I then went to the local store and bought me two forty two ounces of beer and sat right there in the parking lot and drank both of them, so I could just cope with Edward when I got home.

Tammy Ann had no idea about my drinking. I never told her because I did not want her to be ashamed of me, as I was ashamed of myself for the decision I had already made by marrying Edward. I finally got home and when I drove up he did not even get up as he saw me coming up the dirt path to even unlock the back door, he just sat there in his chair ignoring me. Instead of him getting up and asking me if I had a good time or that he had missed me the first thing and only thing he said to me is "Michelle did you see that water bill you have to pay?" I tried really hard ignoring Edward as Tammy Ann told me to do, but Tammy Ann did not know just how hard it was to ignore ignorance, and that was Edward. Little by little, my love for Edward was escaping; the more he treated me like someone that I absolutely hated the more I began to resent him. The more he said such ugly and nasty things about my children the more I was finding myself to dislike him even more. I used to beg him for kisses and hugs but I was starting to fall asleep on the couch and not wanting to share a bed with him at all. Edward was a miserable person and who ever was around him if they were not miserable when they started talking to him, afterwards they were miserable and felt sorry for me.

Soon after, Meghan needing my help Jordan then needed my help, he did not have a place to stay, and when I asked, Edward if he could come and stay with us he said no so fast it would make your head would spin. I told Edward before we ever got married that God did not make a man more perfect than what he made my children, so in other words if Edward thought he would become more important than what my children were then he was seriously wrong. So, by Edward telling me that Jordan could not come back and live with me, I went and got a credit card in both of our names. I got Jordan a place to live in Jacksonville, North Carolina, and we had a credit limit of twelve thousand dollars on the credit card. I made sure my son Jordan had everything he needed in his new home, dishes, electric, cable and even helped him with gas and food.

Since Edward told me I needed a part time job I got myself into a scam on the computer that cost me over six thousand dollars, and I did all of this behind Edward's back or without his knowledge. When the bills would come in I would pay them but it got to the point I could not pay them because of the scam I got myself in. I did not know how to tell Edward but he found out because the creditor called Edward at his job and as soon as he found out he called home and the first people he accused was my children Justin and Jordan.

I tried to explain all of this to him on the phone however; he did not want to hear any of it.

So, when I called Tammy Ann, explained it all to her, and told her that Edward was at Raleigh. I also told Tammy Ann that I was sorry about all of it and if money was not all Edward talked about I would never in my life would have joined this stuff you are suppose to get rich for selling products on the computer I had no idea it was a scam. Tammy Ann knew what I was saying as I was explaining it to her, because that is all Edward would talk about is me going to go to work in some place, when he knew I could not do that because of my MS. However, to Edward that did not even matter. As I drove to Raleigh where Edward was and finally finding the hotel where he was staying I went to his room and tried to explain, he was so drunk and so angry there was no reasoning with him. It was raining so hard outside and instead of him asking me to stay, he told me to leave. It was so hard to get home because the rain was so hard it was extremely hard to see. I finally made it home when it should have only taken me two hours it took me four hours to make it home. Edward did not even call me that week, even though I tried calling him several times and he would not answer his phone.

Finally, it was getting to Thursday night time for him to come home, he got home really late, and when he came in, he did not say anything to me. Of course, I was already used to all of that. That whole weekend he did not speak to me. Edward did not even want to hear why I did what I did and was not interested in it whatsoever. I tried over and over to explain to him why I had done what I had done but Edward was not interested in hearing me at all.

I told him he should have never said my son could not come and live here, that I would never allow any of my children to live on the street. When I said that Edward began to show extremely abusive behavior towards me and told me I was not worth the air I breathed. After saying them harsh words to me, he then said not one of my children was allowed to ever come to his home again. I then said Edward what are you saying? Are you telling me I cannot have any kind of relationship with my children except by telephone, he then said to me your lucky to even have that. At this point, I had nothing more to say to him, and I went to my bedroom and locked the door and when I did that, he kicked the door in and broke it.

Then he went to my best friend's house and told her something and I have no idea what he said but he told me that Tammy Ann threw me under the bus. When he said that I called her and asked her, how could she do that to me? I was yelling from the top of my lungs at my best friend, accusing her of what Edward had said to me. When I did that, I hurt Tammy Ann so deeply, that it broke up our long friendship all because of Edward. It was as if I believed Edward over Tammy Ann when all Tammy Ann had done all during our friendship and was always there for me when Edward was never there for me.

Tammy Ann just was not my best friend she was my family, her husband Brent and her children were my family, and Tammy Ann's Mother and Father treated me as their daughter also. Tammy Ann and I were as close as sisters, she knew everything about me, all my secrets, all my past, and she never judged me. So when I lost her friendship it was like I lost part of my heart due to Edward and that is just what Edward wanted. So, this made Edward very happy, because then he knew I had no one, not one person in my life except him. Little by little, I was losing everything I loved and needed in my life. So, after that it did not take long after losing my very best friend that I became an alcoholic, and I was falling apart very quickly. I was so depressed that I did not even want to wake up in the mornings and when I did the very first thing I did was take my nerve medicine, and my pain medication and then I started drinking, and I would drink all day, while Edward was gone all during the week.

I had absolutely no one, no one to talk to, no one to share my life with, just no one. Edward was happy about this because he knew then all I could do is stay right there at that house in the woods. While Edward was gone out of town for the four days, all I would do is drink and drink. I never hardly ever ate and did not want to eat. I was so sad, so miserable, and when I lost my best friend, it seemed as my whole world had ended. Tammy Ann was like my children's second Mother, and I was like her children's second Mother, I lost it all. When I would get drunk, I would get up enough nerve to try and call Tammy Ann but she never answered. When that would happen all I would do is cry and cry hard. I missed her so much she was the only one in my whole entire life that was my best friend and stood behind me so many times. In my life I tried to have friends, even tried to buy friends and as a child, I even tried doing that as well by giving them my ice cream money, which that never worked either. I had lots of pretend friends but they really did not care about me but Tammy Ann was so different. She was my real friend without wanting anything from me. Tammy Ann just loved who I was just how I was.

When I would talk to Edward about being lonely even when he was home, it did not matter to him. When I lost my very best friend I could only think of the two darkest times in my life, the first one of me losing my daughter Angel, the second one was losing my very best friend Tammy Ann. Edward saw me being so depressed, and being so lonely not having no one in my life. When trying to talk about this to Edward, he did not care and all he said is you brought all this on yourself, and you deserved everything you have got. Edward would never comfort me, even talk me and when I needed to be hugged he did not do that either. Edward would just sit on the computer most of the days while being home on the three days he was off. If he was not on the computer he would go outside and walk around the house over and over, Edward did not want to communicate with me what so ever. Then if Edward would talk to me it was when he was drunk and the things he would say never made any sense to me. After him, drinking so much it would always go back to the same subject and that was my children. Then if it were not the topic of my children then he would bring up all my faults, and especially the credit card I obtained while we were married. Edward made me make every payment to the credit card, and he also knew I had to make my car payment and to pay insurance, then on top of all things; I was forced to pay him rent to be able to stay with him. After doing all of that, he knew I had no money left.

When Edward was home on the three days while he was off if he had to go anywhere the first thing he would do is grab my keys and drive my car but Edward never paid one payment on the car that belonged to me. If I did have gas in my car, he would run it out and never would he replace the gas that was in my car. Edward did not want to drive his truck because his truck was very unreliable and very ugly and completely a dirty mess. Edward never believed in washing his truck, or anything he owned. Edward was a lazy person; he never helped me clean the home, or anything in the home. Edward had hurt me so many times and not one time did he ever say to me he was sorry, and because of that I knew Edward was never sorry for his behavior, the things he said about my children, or the names he called me, or how he acted towards me. Edward showed me no love any at all.

When I would cry my cat 'key key' and my little dog 'Molly' would know I was upset and those little animals would try and comfort me and my dog Molly would lick my tears away. My key key would take his little face and rub it against mine. Those animals knew I was hurt and my heart was broken, and my sweet animals would do all they could to comfort me as best as they could. If it was not for them, I just do not know what I would have done. My animals showed me more attention than what my own husband would do for me. When I would cry all Edward would do is try to make it worse as usual, after the three days he was home, and when Sunday came, I was so happy because I knew the next day he would be gone from the home for four days and nights. Never did Edward tell me he loved me on his own, and I truly believe he never loved me at all, because if he loved me he would have treated me better and be a better husband and try to do better by my children, but Edward did not like it when my children would even come and see me. Eventually Edward got his way and everything and everyone that mattered to me, he got them out of my life. Before being with Edward I was a strong person, a great Mother and lived a good life and had friends, and having a very best friend Tammy Ann. Not to mention I had my own home, which was so great because I lived right next door to my very best friend Tammy Ann. In just four years Edward ran everyone I loved away and not in my life, and ran my children to Georgia, just like Tammy Ann said he would do. I lost everything and this was one of the darkest times of my life. I had no one, including Edward. The days without everyone I loved was so hard, and it got to the point that when Edward was out of town he did not even call me like he used to do.

Chapter 18 Finding Peace In My Storms

In all of my life I have never been this low except for the time I lost my daughter Angel, I knew when I lost my precious daughter who I loved with all my heart my life went down so quickly, and this is something I did not want to happen again. So as I was sitting there at that home while Edward was gone and having no one and becoming an alcoholic very quickly and not only that smoking marijuana as much as I could. I was losing weight from not eating and when I looked in the mirror I saw a person I did not even recognize and a person I did not like at all, I saw a person that was lonely, sad and a person that aged so badly in just a few years from drinking and smoking weed.

When I compared the pictures of me of two years prior to the current date I looked horrible. I felt horrible; everything in my life was horrible. I wanted a life that was different, I did not know how to do this, but I knew God, and I decided to start going to church, when I told this to Edward he laughed and said there is no God and I am wasting my time. Edward did not want anything that might change the person I had become. Edward liked that my life was at a place that was terrible; he did not want anything to change of how I was feeling about myself. Edward wanted me to think I was useless and not worthy of anything good and he especially did not want me to find happiness.

Edward did not want me to go to church and he made that quite clear to me, and said to me if I did this, he would not like this at all. At this point I really did not care about anything he would say, all I knew is I had to get out of the darkness I was in because I knew me better than anyone knew me. I was getting to the point I did not want to live any longer, I had already lost everything that was good in my life. Edward loved the control he had on me and wanted that control to continue, he never supported anything I wanted to do. So one Sunday I decided to go to church, and after that day and hearing the message my brother Joe talked about made me want to go and hear more of what he was saying about God.

My brother Joe really did not want me there because I could tell by his actions, but his daughter and his son and his wife and his Mother In Law were really happy to see me there. So I did not care what Joe felt, I was there only there to hear the message in his sermon. My brother Joe had became a great preacher however some of the things he would say I did not understand, so when I would get home I would look up some of the things he was talking about. I was very proud of my brother for what he was doing, he also helped men that were in trouble with alcohol and drugs and had a program for these men that were quite successful. My brother Joe made these men go to church, which was part of his program in order to get these men help. I never talked to my brother about my drug and alcohol problems, because once again I did not want any of my family to know anything about my life or what Edward was doing to me.

As my brother Joe was building on to his church, he asked me to ask Edward to help him in the electrician part. So when I went home I asked Edward and he did agree to help my brother Joe. The only thing I did not like about some of my Brother Joe's sermons he would often use his family members as examples and especially Joe would use me, which made me very uncomfortable because I did not want the whole church to know my past or my past mistakes. Later on going to his church, I found out from many people that came up to me and told me, so many stories that he had told other people so many stories of my past. To me I felt that was very unprofessional, and it hurt me when I would hear it from others. I felt since my brother Joe was a Pastor he should be the very first person to forgive but I felt as if he never has forgiven me of my past mistakes, and when he hugged me he did the same as my Mother did by giving me a one arm hug. My brother Joe was a Pastor and he enjoyed helping so many people but he could not even see how much his own family was so apart in so many ways. To me I felt like this was something he should work on first, by helping his own family because to me there were so many problems with our own family before helping all the others. My Mother had such hatred in her own heart, my Father was one that held such grudges, and would never let them go. My younger sister also was very unhappy and showed no forgiveness in her own heart and also held such grudges as my Mother did when she as well had so many skeletons in her own closet. My family had such distance and we did not even act like a family. In my brothers Joe's program of helping young boys and also older men with their addictions there were a couple of boys got really close to me. They showed me much attention, and would call me and that was fine with me because I enjoyed being like a Mother to these young boys. However, when my brother Joe saw them getting close to me, he did not like that and he was very jealous of that. When this happened my brother Joe resented this so much more with me, and did not like these young men coming to me instead of him and talking to him. I told these young men that were much not older than my own children they should have been talking to him about their mistakes; I talked to these young men the same as I would do if they were my own sons. I will admit I got very close to these two young men and I treated the boys if they were my own children.

    So once again, I was having more chaos in my life even when I was searching for peace in church so desperately. I had been going to my brother Joe's church now for three months, and was starting to feel better about myself and feeling peace within my own life until this happened. Not only did this make my brother upset it made his wife upset and before I knew it I got phone calls from each of them, telling me to stay away from them boys whom I loved as my own children. I did not understand that at all. Especially one of the boys telling me he had been asking for a bible for a very long time, and not getting one. So, one day I went and got this young man a bible and took it to him, this made this young man so happy and he hugged me so tight with so much appreciation that I did this for him.

    However, to give him the bible I had to go to the building where my brother Joe housed these individuals. I did not know I was not allowed to go there. I left after only staying for about ten minutes. My phone started ringing off the hook, first from my brother Joe, and next his wife who was really ugly and said some words that I did not feel she should of said when all I was doing was delivering a bible to a young man that asked for it and needed it. So once again my family that was Christians hurt me or should I say suppose to be Christians, this hurt me badly when I was searching for peace in my own life.

    So I never went back to his church since and nor do I ever plan too. So again, Edward thought he had won once again, after all, of this I decided to just do my own studying in my own bible, and if I had a question, I would go on the computer to get my answers. Also, after that I did not have anything else to say to my brother's family as well. After all, of this that had happened them two boys still called me and told me things that my own brother who was a Preacher said about me. This hurt me to the core because I could not believe that he would do something like that since he was a Preacher and taking an oath to be a Preacher, but during church and as a part as his sermon he would talk about his own sister. I also went to my brother Joe for help about Edward and told them I was being abused, I needed a safe haven and asked him if I could just come and sleep on his floor, but the answer was NO! Matter of fact my sister-in-law who is my brother Joe's wife told me I got myself into this and I should be able to get myself out of this after her knowing Edward took everything from me including money so just how in the world was I suppose to get out of this horrific situation.

    As the days went by after this situation, it did not make my life any better, I still continued drinking and at the same time I was reading the bible, trying to find and reach my answers and why was all these horrible things that have took place during my entire life. I so desperately wanting my life to change, I wanted to stop drinking and I also wanted to stop smoking marijuana as well, I prayed all during my life but it seemed to me that my prayers did not never reach the ceilings. It seemed to me since I was twelve years of age God did not hear not one prayer of my life. I would pray about my family that never got better. I would pray about Angel, and she got taken away from me. I would pray about so many things in my life and it just seemed nothing got answered. So, this time I was going to give it another shot, I started praying once again before going to sleep and when I would drink a beer I started feeling the feelings of guilt, and I knew these feelings were coming from God. If I started smoking some marijuana, I even started feeling bad about that as well, and I knew that also was coming from God. So I began to start feeling better about things that were happening about my life. If I heard of a Christian event that was happening in our small town, I would attend. Things were changing and I was finding myself becoming happier, more understanding, I was even finding myself not crying as much as what I used to.

    My life as far as Edward had not changed he was still his hateful self, cursing as he usually did, and making fun of me as usual, but things were not bothering me like they once did. Edward noticed that things were changing about me as well, and I was moving forward in my life, which was something he did not like.

It was becoming tax time and I needed to know how his employer's filed him this year as being single or being married. I called his employer's and when the secretary answered the phone and I told her who I was and when I told her I was Michelle Price and that, I was Edward's wife. The secretary then said to me she did not even know Edward was even married. When that happened I was driving a vehicle and when this was taking place and when that woman told me this, I almost wrecked the car. I could not believe this at all. Just when I was beginning to feel better about things once again, he destroyed everything I was working on. Once again I felt worthless, felt as if I was not worth trash you would throw away, once again I felt as if he was completely ashamed of me just one more time.

All the horrible things that I carried in my heart and in my head just came flooding back once again. I felt so unloved as I have most of my life, and all the way home all I did was cry till I got home. As I was approaching home I did not want Edward to see that I had been crying so I dried my face off, and again being the great actress I have had to be all my life I acted as if nothing was wrong. Once I pulled in the driveway driving down the path to our home, I saw Edward outside starting the grill because he was going to cook something on the outdoor grill. As I got out of the car, I acted as if nothing was wrong with me, as I was walking up the steps Edward said did you call my job. I said yes, I needed to know about our taxes and how you filed. Then he said so you know they did not know I was married, I said yes I found that out also and then I asked him why did he do that?

Then I said Edward do you know how bad that made me feel? Then I also said Edward I felt like an idiot because we have been married now a year and not even your job knew you were married. When you worked with your Co-workers that just verified everything I always have thought, number one you have been taking off your ring all day and put it back on when you came home, and second you are ashamed that I am your wife, and then I walked into the house crying. It took a while before Edward would even come into the house because once again he knew he had hurt me and hurt me badly. When he did come in, I said Edward when you took them days off when we got married what did you tell your employer. Edward said with this straight and cold look on his face and said I told them I was just taking a vacation. I said really?

He then said Michelle please do not start your crap again, I already told you I did not want people in my business. I thought to myself what in the world. Who in the world would care if Edward got married or not? The only person that cared was himself. Edward showed me on many occasions that he did not want to be married he just loved having someone there to cook for him, clean for him and someone to decorate his home which I thought was suppose to be our home. This hurt me so badly that night I slept on the couch that night with my dog Molly and my cat Key Key slept in the chair next to me. I just got sick and tired of Edward's excuses of not loving me, being ashamed of me and how he made me feel as a human being, and never once even getting I am a sorry from him.

So, the next morning when he left to go to work he did not kiss me bye and when he tried to call me during the day I did not even answer the phone. I had so much to think about and what I was going to do. Edward had to go out of town and stay gone four days for his job, that made me very happy because I needed that time without him to think about what I was going to do and when I was going to be able to do it. All I know I was tired of having to beg him to love me, hug me, kiss me and most importantly showing me I mattered to him.

While Edward was gone during those four days, I decided to go to Georgia and visit my children, and was even thinking moving there where they were. I missed my children so badly, when my son Jordan told me when he moved from North Carolina to move to Georgia he said he cried the whole way to Georgia, after hearing that it broke my heart, I felt like I had let my children down so badly, and became a person that they did not even know. My children knew me as a very strong person someone that they admired so much, but after Edward, they did not even recognize me. I was a sad person, a person that cried so often, a person that allowed to be mentally abused, and emotionally abused, and when they saw this they could not understand because while raising my children I was a strong, spoke my mind, and always stood up for myself, and when Edward came in my life, it all changed. I began to feel bad about myself, never had my children seen this from me.

While I was in Georgia, my son Jordan said to me he would make a deposit on a house and for me to move there where all my children were. My children and I went looking to find a rental that was big enough for the four of us. We found one and it was so pretty. It had a pond several decks and the rent was five hundred dollars a month with a deposit of five hundred dollars. Jordan said he would pay the deposit and he did, so when I left Georgia to go back to North Carolina I was all set to move to Georgia where my children were. When I made this decision to move back to Georgia my children were extremely happy about my decision, but deep down I was miserable, even though they did not like Edward and how he did their Mother I loved Edward and still wanted to try and make this marriage work.

Instead of crying all the way from North Carolina to Georgia, I cried all the way from Georgia to North Carolina. I was so sad, and all the way driving back home to North Carolina, Edward had called my cell phone so many times but not once did I ever answer. I did not have anything to say to him, he had hurt me so badly, and he acted, as he really did not care any at all. I arrived home from Georgia, without Edward knowing I had taken this trip. I walked into our home after the trip I just looked at all the pictures of Edward and myself hanging on the wall. When I looked at these pictures I would just cry and I would just ask God why he did not love me. I prayed to God what I have done that made him not show me any love or affection, asking God why he married me if he did not love me.

I knew I loved Edward so much and was willing to try and make this marriage work; I would often stare out the kitchen window and pray to God to take either him or me. But praying for God to take me because I knew I was saved and he was not, and I knew if God took him he would not go to heaven. Edward was not happy and I knew that and I did everything I could do to change this but no matter what I did, it never changed. So before Edward came home my MS started acting up, I was finding that my legs were not working the way they should, and I was so stressed out and that is why my MS started acting up. Stress is the worse thing for MS but Edward did not even care about that.

So that Wednesday before Edward was due home on that Thursday, I just laid on the couch all day resting and trying as hard as I could to not think about what was going on in my life. I would pray and pray and hoping God was hearing my prayers. I dreaded to know Edward was coming home the next day, I never knew what kind of mood he would be in when he would come home. Edward was always a person that complained about everything, Edward never seemed happy about anything. I could not understand that because he had so much to be thankful for. His home was paid for and he had no mortgage. His land was paid for and he also had a rental home, which he made more money each month from renting out his single wide. He had a wife that cleaned, cooked, and did everything, so that when he got home he had nothing to do except what he wanted to do. He also had thousands of dollars in the bank. I knew so many people would have loved to be in his place but Edward was so miserable about everything when he had every reason to be happy. Edward had no worries, he was in a position in his life that he should have been very thankful, but he was not. Edward did not believe in God, and made fun of me for doing so, while I was lying on the couch trying to rest, I played all these thoughts in my head over and over. Just what was I going to do? So I decided when Edward would come home we would talk, and I was going to tell him my plans of moving to Georgia.

Chapter 19 Postponing my move

That whole day on Thursday my stomach was so nervous that I felt sick; I was also very scared of how this was going to work, and what he would say. As I stood at that kitchen window waiting on Edward to drive up the path to our home, eventually I saw him coming up the path and I was sort of beside myself. After seeing him coming up the path, I quickly went into the living room and sat on the couch as if I had been watching the television the whole time. When Edward walked in, he said "hello." I replied I am in here. Edward knew by me not talking to him from not seeing him the entire week the entire week he was gone for his job that I was really hurt. So, when he came into house he took off his shoes and then came into the living room. He didn't even stop and get a beer first. Then he bent down hugged and kissed me. When Edward did that I was all confused again, thinking maybe he had learned a lesson and he knew just how badly he had hurt me. After him doing that he then sat in his chair and asked me how my week went, I did not have much to say but deep down I wanted to say a whole lot, but after he hugged me and kissed me, I waited on telling him my plans. I did tell him that my MS started acting up and told him that it was from the stress he had put me through from the week before.

Edward then got real quite and just held his head down and did not say he was sorry to me once again. I then asked Edward was he ashamed of me and he looked at me and said NO. I then asked him then why did he not tell his employer he was married. Edward gave me the same excuse as he did before he left and that was he did not like people in his business. I then said Edward who in the world would care if you got married or not? Why would you hide that unless you were ashamed of me? I also said to him do you actually know how that makes me feel. I then said Edward before we left to get married I told everyone that we were going to get married. I then told Edward he has met every one of my friends, my family and all I have met in your life was just your family. I did not know any of your friends and you have never taken me to meet any of your friends this whole time. As soon as I started telling him all of this, he then got up, went into the kitchen, and got a beer. That is when I knew he did not want to hear any more of what I wanted to say, so I just remained quiet as he got on the computer as he usually did once he got home.

As he did that I went into the kitchen, got a beer, just stood at that window in the kitchen, and just looked outside as I did so often when I had so much on my mind. I was sad and once again, I felt as I was living the life as I did when I was a kid. When things went wrong in my Mother and Father's marriage or in our family instead of talking and working things out everything just got swept under the rug and nothing ever got resolved which made everyone feel as if we all were all walking on egg shells and afraid to say anything. This was a life that I never wanted, and was one of the reasons I left home at such a tender age of fifteen and never going back to live there.

When I raised my three children on my own we always had a very open relationship between us four, we would talk no matter of any circumstances, the good the bad and the ugly. I never wanted my children to feel as if they could not come to me and talk to me for any reason. I just stood there at that window drinking one beer after another just trying to figure out what I was going to do. I barely said anything to Edward that night and he barely said anything to me after he got home that night. I tried so many times and very often to talk to Edward about our problems and about my feelings but he would never want to talk and especially never wanting to talk about his feelings. The more I thought about our marriage the more I saw how my marriage was beginning to be just like my Mother and Father's marriage, and that was something I did never want in my life.

Not to mention how I was drinking to the point that I was drinking beer from the time I got up until the time I went to bed, slowly but surely, I was becoming my Father. The more I drank the more I understood why my Father would drink like he did when I was a child. It was because of my Mother and how she was never happy, never satisfied about anything in her own life. I was living with a person just like my Mother and that was Edward. I could not believe I had become an alcoholic just like my Father. I have had many problems during my life: not being loved by my family, losing my daughter Angel then raising my three children on my own, and going through several divorces. But, never had I turned to alcohol to help me deal with any of these problems, even when I got sick with MS, and losing everything and having to file bankruptcy did I ever turn to alcohol, so I started asking myself why am I doing this now?

Why did I have to have alcohol just to function? I was so lonely, my children had left and were grown, I was married, but I was so lonely as if I had no one in my life, even though I was married to Edward. Even when Edward was home it was still as if he was at work because when he was home we never talked and we barely made love any at all. I never got any affection from Edward any more after we got married. Edward never said anything nice to me but that day when he came in and hugged me and kissed me after he knew he had hurt me I knew it was just his way of saying he was sorry even though he never spoke the words to me. Later on that evening, I fixed our dinner and as usual, Edward was still on the computer. It was nothing for him to stay on it for several hours at a time and often all day when he was off from work. I took his plate that I fixed for dinner to where he was at the computer and he often sat their at that desk and ate his dinner. When he would finish his dinner I would go to the desk and get his plate, so I could wash the dishes. Even after doing all of this I never even, got a thank you. I would clean the kitchen up and come back into the living room and never did we ever talk, it was three days of feeling like I was nothing to him but his cook, house cleaner and just someone to satisfy his needs.

That night preparing to go to bed, I did not even sleep with Edward that night; I slept in the room that used to be Jordan's. I did not get much sleep because I had so very much on my mind. I was debating on leaving Edward, but I knew I would have to tell him, and not just leave while he was at work because I felt like that would be a coward thing to do. So while I laid there in that bed that night I tossed and tossed knowing I loved Edward but also knowing Edward did not love me, and if I changed my mind of not leaving then once again I would be hurting my children and I did not want that either. I was once again in a bad situation.

When I married Edward, I meant every word I said that day, and deep down in my heart I did not want to leave Edward, I truly loved Edward but I hated his ways, and how he treated me. There were days that he treated me so good, but more often than not, he treated me badly. But once again, I thought I could talk to Edward telling him my feelings and telling him if things did not change then I would be leaving. It seemed like every time I would bring this up, all he said is all I wanted was what he had and that was all I wanted to do is take him to the bank. By that, he thought that I was planning on getting alimony and anything I could from him. When in reality and also so many times I said to him all I wanted from him was just his love and nothing more, and besides I told him that everything that was in our home already belong to me to begin with.

Edward knew that but Edward had a real problem loving money more than anything else in his life. Edward loved money more than he loved his own Mother. There were so many things about Edward that I did not understand or the things he would never want to talk about while being a child or things about our marriage. To me if you did not talk about the issues that were at hand then how could anything be fixed or resolved, they could not be. I just could not understand why Edward did not want people to know he had married me. There were several other issues that bothered me and they were when this lady named Constance that lived right down from Edward came to his single wide on two different occasions and he had already rented this home out by then but this lady came to the renter's door and asked for Edward by his name.

This lady Constance was a very nasty lady and had been a prostitute in her life, been jailed many times from drugs and other stuff. She had also lost all four of her children to the state for being a very unfit mother. She lived in a house that had no electricity, or water and she was a full blown drug addict and alcoholic. Edward claimed he did not know her but if he did not know her then how did she know his name. And, how did she know to come to that house and ask for him if he did not know her? By this time, I was finding more and more things out about Edward. He either messed around with married women or messed with women that had no morals. Edward wanted to have a girl but without any commitment. Edward I believe that is what Edward wanted from me from the beginning however I was not that type of girl and he knew that. Edward knew he had to marry me or he would have to go back to the life we both had before knowing each other and I do not think he wanted that.

So, the next morning when we woke up he asked me why did I not sleep with him last night. I told him that I had a whole lot of things on my mind. Edward then knew by my actions all day that our relationship and marriage were in real trouble. Every weekend Edward was home the only thing we did together was to go to the grocery store and that was it, we had no entertainment what so ever. We never went anywhere unless I planned it and paid for it. I was broke and barely had enough money to even get me through each month after paying my bills. Edward not putting me on his insurance to help me out only meant that I got more and more bills, which he refused to, help me pay.

Edward would receive bonuses all during the year, and on top of it he claimed me on his taxes and when the tax refund came back in both of our names he deposited the whole check into his account, and never gave me a dime of it. The whole I was with Edward he never bought me one outfit, no under garments or anything. But, because of me, he had a whole closet full of new clothes to work in so that when he went to work he would look nice and professional. Right down to his work coat to his work boots, it was me getting him all of these things, but when it came to me, he did not buy me anything or care if I had anything.

The more I got to know Edward the more I began to know just how selfish Edward was, and how it was all about him and no one else. Edward said to me on many occasions that the reason he never had children was because he could not afford children, later on during our marriage I found out that was not the reason, the reason was it was because he had the love of money way more than he had love of anything or anyone.

After knowing all these things about Edward, I was still trying to change him, show, and teach him how to love and how to treat people, like how a lot of women try and do. So, after me cooking breakfast that morning and we ate and after me, cleaning the kitchen up I told Edward we needed to talk. He then said what is there to talk about. I said Edward there is a whole lot to talk about, and as usual he was on the computer, so I asked him to get off the computer so we could talk and he did but he really did not want to because I could tell by his behavior. Edward was acting like a two year old when you would take his toy truck away. Eventually I started telling him all my thoughts concerns and especially how tired I was of how our marriage was going and what was going on with our marriage. I told him I have to beg him for affection, I was showed no love, and that when he came in from work he never acted happy to see me. I told him how I resented him talking very harsh words against my children, I also told him I was sad, and I was lonely that when he was home all he did was stay on the computer. I reminded him that he never did anything with me or for me. He then said that he did do things for me. I asked him what he did. Edward said I pay for the cable, electric, water and the phones, I looked at him and said Edward, and you would have to pay for those things if I were here or not.

Then I said some things are going to have to change, I said Edward you do not even make love to me any longer, and then he said the reason he did not do that was because I always had this sad look on my face, and I never acted happy. Then I said Edward who would be happy that when we are together we never go out and eat, we never do anything fun because your as tight as a bark on a tree with your money when you have thousands and thousands in the bank. I then asked him what I could do to save this marriage.

Edward never gave me an answer nor did he ask me what he could do to save this marriage. However, he did tell me he loved me. Edward knew I had about had enough of his actions, deceit, and being ashamed of me without cause, so that night he called in a seafood dinner but he only ordered one plate and that was where we could split it. I just could not believe it, that he was so cheap he could not even order two plates of seafood. Edward also went to the liquor store, got some liquor, and also had gotten some beer. So, after eating, he fixed us a drink and before it, we both were feeling the alcohol, this whole time Edward knew what he was doing, because when we went to bed and he started kissing me and that was something that we had not done in many months. In no time were having sex, and it was always the same. Just a little kissing, no foreplay and I always had to be on top, I maybe went up and down three to four times then it was over, he had finished and there was nothing more. It had been like this since being together. I did all the work and he just lay there, he would not even get up to wash. I even had to bring him a wash cloth to wash and I even had to wash him. After that, instead of him hugging me and kissing me, he just turned over and went straight to sleep. That is what I call just sex. I felt so low, was even ashamed of myself, and felt like I was nothing but a whore because to me that was not making love. It was like having sex with a complete stranger and it was terrible.

I so often would cry myself to sleep after having sex with him, which was very rarely. I would think each time when we would make love, it would be different but it never changed nor did it ever get better. My heart broke every time. After doing that with Edward, I felt so belittled, so unwanted and very much unworthy, he never rubbed my body, my hair, or even showed me love. It was just about his satisfaction but by getting his satisfaction made me feel even more horrible about myself.

Later that night after doing that I could not go to sleep, I needed comfort, and I opened my bible up to read how a marriage is supposed to be. I was trying to find my peace, and praying to God asking Him what to do when it came to this marriage. I knew deep down that this marriage was not getting any better. Most of all I wanted my life to be different by not drinking any more. I begged God to take the taste away, and prayed to God to give me a sign in what I needed to do for myself to make myself feel better about whom I was as a person.

So, as I was reading God was speaking to me so clearly, he told me to start writing what bothered me and what has hurt me during my life. I have had so much hurt in my life and God knew I could help so many others from the hurt I have experienced in my own life. I never had much confidence in myself and especially what God was telling me to do but I always had a diary even when I was little, and I enjoyed writing very much, but I never thought any would be interested in what I had been through much less be interested in what has happened during my own life. So, as I was falling asleep God was talking to me just as clear, just as I was having a conversation as I would that was here on earth. It was so clear, and something I was willing to try. When I told God I would do this, he told me this is what he wanted me to do, and to have faith, because he would make sure every book that I would write would be a complete success.

The next morning when I woke up, I felt different, so renewed, and most importantly so loved by a power I could not explain. As Edward was leaving to go to work that morning I started writing and I wrote all day just as God wanted me to do, and during this time God gave me all my answers that I had from years ago, and from that day forward my mind has been so clear. I knew what God wanted from me, that was to write my story of my life so I can help others out in the world that need help like I did in my own life. After doing this, I felt so wonderful knowing God had a plan for me.

Chapter 20 Doing as God wanted Writing my Books of Pain to help others

That morning my mind was so crystal clear of everything I needed to do, it was October of 2011 and I started my very first book, and God had already gave me the title of this first book and the name of it is "Lies In The Womb." This book is about all the pain I endured from my Mother who stole my first daughter Angel away from me. It was about the pain that I went through while raising my other three children all on my own. God gave me this story and I as I started writing it I had to go way back in time and discover evidence that I never thought existed from the courts, since it had been so long ago. Also, when I was doing my research, I also found many things in the bible as well; of how a marriage is, suppose to be. Also, how parents were suppose to be to their children as well. As I was reading my bible, I came across these verses in the bible that gave me much comfort and I want to share them with you.

This verse was in Psalms 27:10-14

Even if my Mother and Father abandon me,

The Lord will hold me close.

Teach me how to live Oh Lord

Lead me on the path of honesty,

For my enemies are waiting for me to fall.

Do not let me fall into their hands.

For they have accused me of things, I have never done

And breathe out violence against me.

Yet, I am confident that I will see the Lord's goodness

While I am here in the land of the living

Wait patiently for the Lord.

Be brave and courageous.

Yes, wait patiently for the Lord.

When I read that verse in the bible, it gave me such comfort and made me realize how this whole time, God kept me safe even through all my horrible mistakes. How he loved me and kept me safe when no one else loved me on earth but God loved me and God had many plans stored for me when I did not even know that.

My second favorite verse was 1 King 3: 16-28

A Wise Ruling

16 Now two prostitutes came to the king and stood before him.

17 One of them said, "Pardon me, my lord. This woman and I live in the same house, and I had a baby while she was there with me.

18 The third day after my child was born, this woman also had a baby. We were alone; there was no one in the house but the two of us.

19 "During the night this woman's son died because she lay on him.

20 So she got up in the middle of the night and took my son from my side while I your servant was asleep. She put him by her breast and put her dead son by my breast.

21 The next morning, I got up to nurse my son—and he was dead! But when I looked at him closely in the morning light, I saw that it wasn't the son I had borne."

22 The other woman said, "No! The living one is my son; the dead one is yours."

But the first one insisted, "No! The dead one is yours; the living one is mine." And so, they argued before the king.

23 The king said, "This one says, 'My son is alive and your son is dead,' while that one says, 'No! Your son is dead and mine is alive.'"

24 Then the king said, "Bring me a sword." So, they brought a sword for the king.

25 He then gave an order: "Cut the living child in two and give half to one and half to the other."

26 The woman whose son was alive was deeply moved out of love for her son and said to the king, "Please, my lord, give her the living baby! Don't kill him!"

But the other said, "Neither I nor you shall have him. Cut him in two!"

27 Then the king gave his ruling: "Give the living baby to the first woman. Do not kill him; she is his mother."

28 When all Israel heard the verdict the king had given, they held the king in awe, because they saw that he had wisdom from God to administer justice.

This verse kept me from killing myself, which I tried three times to do. I wanted to die when I lost my first daughter Angel to my Mother who had also lost her first daughter Carrie.

So, many times during my life I felt so alone. I spent many years wanting and searching for love and so many times in my life, having one marriage after another. Seeking so hard to find what I was looking for when the whole time all I was wanting and needing was just love, unconditional love is what I needed and what I have always wanted so badly.

Deuteronomy 4:29-30

29 But if from there you seek the Lord your God, you will find him if you seek him with all your heart and with all your soul.

30 When you are in distress and all these things have happened to you, then in later days you will return to the Lord your God and obey him.

Growing up as a child we did not go to church very often and if we did it was always our Mother taking us, never as a child did I see my Father go to church. All my life I knew God was true because I had this Granny, which was my Father's Grandmother, but she raised my Father so he called her Momma, and to us she was our Granny. This woman did not read or write but she knew the bible. As a child, I would remember things she would say about the bible and this was her verse:

Psalm 33:20-21

20 We wait in hope for the Lord;

He is our help and our shield.

In him our hearts rejoice,

For we trust in his holy name.

The world has changed so much and people have changed because the world has changed but there are so many things that people need to know:

Proverbs 6:16-19

16 There are six things the Lord hates,

Seven that are detestable to him:

Haughty eyes,

A lying tongue,

Hands that shed innocent blood,

A heart that devises wicked schemes,
Feet that are quick to rush into evil,
A false witness who pours out lies
And a person who stirs up conflict in the community.

How to get blessings from God and what to do and ask for:
Matthew 3:1-12
New International Version (NIV)
John the Baptist Prepares the Way

3 In those days John the Baptist came, preaching in the wilderness of Judea 2 and saying, "Repent, for the kingdom of heaven has come near."

This is he who was spoken of through the prophet Isaiah:
"A voice of one calling in the wilderness,
'Prepare the way for the Lord,
Make straight paths for him.'"

4 John's clothes were made of camel's hair, and he had a leather belt around his waist. His food was locusts and wild honey.

5 People went out to him from Jerusalem and all Judea and the whole region of the Jordan.

6 Confessing their sins, they were baptized by him in the Jordan River.

7 But when he saw many of the Pharisees and Sadducees coming to where he was baptizing, he said to them: "You brood of vipers! Who warned you to flee from the coming wrath?

8 Produce fruit in keeping with repentance.

9 And do not think you can say to yourselves, 'We have Abraham as our father.' I tell you that out of these stones God can raise up children for Abraham.

10 The ax is already at the root of the trees, and every tree that does not produce good fruit will be cut down and thrown into the fire.

11 "I baptize you with water for repentance. But after me comes one who is more powerful than I, whose sandals I am not worthy to carry. He will baptize you with the Holy Spirit and fire.

12 His winnowing fork is in his hand, and he will clear his threshing floor, gathering his wheat into the barn and burning up the chaff with unquenchable fire."

In this marriage with Edward, I would call him an idiot but when I saw this in the bible, I knew I was doing no better than the names he was and still calling me:

Matthew 5:22

22 But I tell you that anyone who is angry with a brother or sister will be subject to judgment. Again, anyone who says to a brother or sister, 'Raca,' is answerable to the court. And anyone who says, 'You fool!' will be in danger of the fire of hell.

While doing my research of how God can fix all problems I came across this verse that now is one of my favorite verses:

Matthew 7:7

Ask, Seek, Knock

7 "Ask and it will be given to you; seek and you will find; knock and the door will be opened to you.

When I started writing Edward was very curious as to what I was doing and when he asked me, I told him, I am writing a book because God has asked me to. Oh, did he laugh and made fun of me and said all you're doing is writing blank pages. I just ignored everything he said and kept writing and having faith in what God asked me to do.

Finally, after finishing my book Edward wanted to read the book Lies In The Womb, so I allowed him to read it. After he finished reading this book he was angry and he started using the "gd" word not to mention telling me how he would be so ashamed of me if any of his friends read it, and I said what friends? I do not know any of your friends so how would they know I was the Author. Then Edward replied well I am sure no one will want to hear your story or read your book to begin with.

The day came and I got an offer from this publishing company called Tate Publishing which was a Christian Publishing company and when I told Edward this he told me that if I did this then I needed to go live with God and as soon as he said that I said, "Amen that is my plan." I had been saving every cent I could get and when he found that out he went to my Brother Joe's home to find out where I was getting the money. I told him, if you do this when you get back I will not be here. As he was leaving, I was leaving also. Edward erratically went down the driveway. I was scared and I knew he was going to ruin whatever small relationship I had been working on so hard to re-build with my brother Joe. I knew I had to finally do what I said I would do, and that was to leave and to leave for good this time.

As I was gathering up a few clothes, my dog Molly, my pocketbook I knew I had no money, no place to go, but I knew I had faith that God would give me what I needed. I had a girlfriend who's Father allowed me to stay there until I was able to get my disability check to move to Georgia where my children where. My friend's Father agreed and I stayed there with my friend's Father. While I was in such a hurry to leave my home I had forgotten my medicine and even God supplied that as well, because arriving to my friend's Fathers home he had all the medication I needed for my MS.

That night my MS was acting up very much and I had fell while walking Molly outside, when I got up my left ear was bleeding and I had a dent in my left side of my head. When I went in and my friend's Father saw me, bleeding, and he helped me to clean myself up. He also helped me by giving me some money to buy myself whatever I needed because I came with no gas, no money, and no food for me or my dog, Molly. While I was gone to the store to get what I needed, my friend's Father, who was a Deacon of a church, called his Pastor, and another Pastor he had knew and also another Deacon and his daughter to make sure what he was willing to do was not a sin for him to help me. They all told him there was nothing in the Bible that said it was wrong for him to let me stay in his home or to help me.

Three days after leaving Edward I received my contract from Tate Publishing and have been on a book tour now six months. God did this all of this, due to me having faith in him. God is amazing and he has taken care of me my whole life when I did not even know God. Now, Edward and I are divorced and God has blessed me so very much since depending on God himself. So, I encourage all that are in verbal, emotional, or physical relationships to depend on God and get out of those kinds of relationships because God will never let you down, as he has not let me down once since I have depended on him.

Problems Of Abuse and Statistics

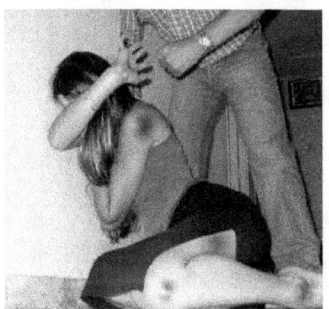

This has happened to me and I have also many other women this has happened to. I do not believe God would want this to happen to you. The first thing you need to do is to start feeling better about yourself because has long as you do not feel good about yourself this will continue happening. When a man tells you he loves you then turns around and hurts you either by mentally, verbally, and physically this is NOT love. This is control. The first time someone hits you, the second time only gets easier. Please believe in yourself and get yourself out of this situation and have Faith in God that he will give you a safe haven as he did for me.

Article Written by: Charles Montaldo

Domestic abuse is a growing problem that affects millions of people in all kinds of relationships including traditional marriages, same-sex partnerships or even relationships where there is no sexual intimacy involved.

Physical violence, of course, is the most blatant form of domestic abuse, sometimes called intimate partner violence. But physical abuse is not the only form of domestic abuse.

Four Main Types of Abuse

According to the Centers for Disease Control and Prevention, intimate partner violence means physical, sexual, or psychological harm inflicted by a current or former spouse or partner.

According to the CDC, these are the four main types of intimate partner violence:

Physical Violence - This mean intentionally using physical force to harm, injuries, disable, or kill. It can involve using a weapon or restrains or merely using body, size, or strength to harm another person. Physical violence can include:

    Burning

    Biting

    Choking

    Grabbing

    Punching

    Pushing

    Throwing

    Scratching

    Shoving

    Shaking

Slapping

Sexual Violence - Sexual abuse not only includes forcing someone to have sex, but it can also include having sex with someone who is unable to refuse due to disability, illness, intimidation or the influence of alcohol or other drugs.

There are three main categories of sexual abuse:

Using physical force to compel someone to have sex against their will, whether the act is completed or not.

Attempting or having sex with someone who is unable to understand the nature of the act or unable to decline participation or is unable to communicate their unwillingness.

Abusive sexual contact of any kind.

Threats of Violence - The use of words, gestures, motions, looks or weapons to communicate a threat to harm, injure, disable, rape or kill them. The act does not have to be carried out for it to be abusive behavior.

Psychological and Emotional Abuse - Using acts, threats of acts or coercive tactics to cause someone emotional trauma. If there has been previous physical or sexual abuse in the relationship, any further threat of abuse is considered psychological or emotion violence.

Psychological abuse can include:

Humiliation

Controlling what the victim can and cannot do.

Withholding information.

Diminishing or embarrassing the victim.

Isolating the victim from friends and family.

Denying the victim access to money or other resources.

Get Help Immediately

Research shows that domestic violence usually gets progressively worse. Rarely does it stop because the abuser promises that it will never happen again. If you are in an abusive relationship, there are many resources available to help you. Please seek help today.

DOMESTIC VIOLENCE FACTS

NCADV Public Policy Office · 1633 Q St NW # 210 · Washington, DC 20009 · (202) 745-1211 · Fax: (202) 745-0088 publicpolicy@ncadv.org

The FINAL Chapter Of ABUSE provides the reader with a look at her lives and all of the various hardships she endured as a result of her poor relationship with her family and the negative impact it can have on a person's entire life. Please visit her page at Michelle at her website http://www.MichelleTaylorMyBooks.com

The FINAL Chapter Of ABUSE is a story of Michelle Taylor searching for love with one abusive relationship after another one including having a very dysfunctional family that showed her no love all of her life. Still today her past haunts her and she has ran from her demons all of her life. This is a book that will tell you about the abuse she endured for years of her life since she was fifteen years of age. She honestly shares her story so she can help others that have gone through the same kind of abuse she has gone through during their lives.

Carla Whaley

I read your book and I cried for you. I wish for you only the best life has to offer. I truly do not know how you made it to tell your story but I am thankful I got to know you better thru your words. Thanks for signing my book; my Mom and daughter Stacie went to the church since I had to work. Thanks again for telling your story.

Justin Wyatt Taylor

I recently finished reading the book, Lies in the Womb, written, and most importantly, LIVED by a woman I consider a "Modern Day Wonder Woman." She is absolutely sensational. God has delivered her through so much that I'm sure others, including myself, can relate to. She endured so many hardships throughout her life. God had His Divine hands on here the whole entire way, I am confident to say. She is also a dear friend of mine and a mentor to say the least. I recommend anyone and everyone to take a look into her life and see what all God has done for her. Just maybe, I pray, you will better understand the sovereignty of our God through His Son, Jesus Christ. Much love to all! Again, be sure to check out Michelle Taylor's page and story!

Melvin Dixon

Just finished reading a book called "Lies In The Womb," that was written by a friend of mine named Michelle Taylor. It was insightful, motivating and

SEXUAL ASSAULT AND STALKING

One in 6 women and 1 in 33 men have experienced an attempted or completed rape.10
Nearly 7.8 million women have been raped by an intimate partner at some point in their lives.11
Sexual assault or forced sex occurs in approximately 40-45% of battering relationships.12
1 in 12 women and 1 in 45 men have been stalked in their lifetime.13
81% of women stalked by a current or former intimate partner are also physically assaulted by that partner; 31% are also sexually assaulted by that partner.13

CHILDREN WHO WITNESS
Witnessing violence between one's parents or caretakers is the strongest risk factor of transmitting violent behavior from one generation to the next.7
Boys who witness domestic violence are *twice as likely* to abuse their own partners and children when they become adults.8
30% to 60% of perpetrators of intimate partner violence also abuse children in the household.9

HOMICIDE AND INJURY
Almost **one-third of female homicide victims** that are reported in police records are killed by an intimate partner.14
In 70-80% of intimate partner homicides, no matter which partner was killed, the man physically abused the woman before the murder.12
Less than one-fifth of victims reporting an injury from intimate partner violence sought medical treatment following the injury.15
Intimate partner violence results in more than *18.5 million mental health care visits* each year.16

One in every four women will experience domestic violence in her lifetime.1
An estimated 1.3 million women are victims of physical assault by an intimate partner each year.2
85% of domestic violence victims are women.3
Historically, females have been most often victimized by someone they knew.4
Females who are *20-24 years of age* are at the greatest risk of nonfatal intimate partner violence.5
Most cases of domestic violence are never reported to the police.6

DID YOU KNOW?
The cost of intimate partner violence **exceeds $5.8 billion each year**, $4.1 billion of which is for direct medical and mental health services.17

Victims of intimate partner violence *lost almost 8 million days of paid work* because of the violence perpetrated against them by current or former husbands, boyfriends and dates. This loss is the equivalent of more than *32,000 full-time jobs* and almost *5.6 million days of household productivity* as a result of violence.17

There are 16,800 homicides and $2.2 million (medically treated) injuries due to intimate partner violence annually, which costs $37 billion.18

ECONOMIC IMPACT
SOURCES 7/07

1 Tjaden, Patricia & Thoennes, Nancy. National Institute of Justice and the Centers of Disease Control and Prevention, "Extent, Nature and Consequences of Intimate Partner Violence: Findings from the National Violence Against Women Survey,"(2000).

2 Costs of Intimate Partner Violence Against Women in the United States. 2003. Centers for Disease Control and Prevention, National Centers for Injury Prevention and Control. Atlanta, GA.

3 Bureau of Justice Statistics Crime Data Brief, *Intimate Partner Violence, 1993-2001*, February 2003.

4 U.S. Department of Justice, Bureau of Justice Statistics, "Criminal Victimization, 2005,"September 2006.

5 U.S. Department of Justice, Bureau of Justice Statistics, "Intimate Partner Violence in the United States,"December 2006.

6 Frieze, I.H., Browne, A. (1989) Violence in Marriage. In L.E. Ohlin & M. H. Tonry (eds.) *Family Violence*. Chicago, IL: University of Chicago Press.

7 Break the Cycle. (2006). *Startling Statistics*. http://www.breakthecycle.org/html%20files/I_4a_startstatis.htm.

8 Strauss, Gelles, and Smith, "Physical Violence in American Families: Risk Factors and Adaptations to Violence"in *8,145 Families*. Transaction Publishers (1990).

9 Edelson, J.L. (1999). "The Overlap Between Child Maltreatment and Woman Battering."*Violence Against Women*. 5:134-154.

10 U.S. Department of Justice, "Prevalence, Incidence, and Consequences of Violence Against Women,"November 1998.

11 *Costs of Intimate Partner Violence Against Women in the United States*. 2003. Centers for Disease Control and Prevention, National Centers for Injury Prevention and Control. Atlanta, GA.

12 Campbell, et al. (2003). "Assessing Risk Factors for Intimate Partner Homicide."*Intimate Partner Homicide*, NIJ Journal, 250, 14-19. Washington, D.C.: National Institute of Justice, U.S. Department of Justice.

13 Tjaden, Patricia & Thoennes, Nancy. (1998). "Stalking in America."National Institute for Justice.

14 Federal Bureau of Investigation, *Uniform Crime Reports* "Crime in the United States, 2000,"(2001).

15 U.S. Department of Justice, Bureau of Justice Statistics, "Intimate Partner Violence in the United States,"December 2006.

16 *Costs of Intimate Partner Violence Against Women in the United States*. 2003. Centers for Disease Control and Prevention, National Centers for Injury Prevention and Control. Atlanta, GA.

Tjaden, Patricia & Thoennes, Nancy.

17 *Costs of Intimate Partner Violence Against Women in the United States*. 2003. Centers for Disease Control and Prevention, National Centers for Injury Prevention and Control. Atlanta, GA.

18 The Cost of Violence in the United States. 2007. Centers for Disease Control and Prevention, National Centers for Injury Prevention and Control. Atlanta, GA.

19 U.S. Department of Justice, Bureau of Justice Statistics, "Family Violence Statistics,"June 2005.

20 U.S. Department of Justice, Bureau of Justice Statistics, "Criminal Victimization,".

For more information, please visit our website at www.ncadv.org.

States differ on the type of relationship that qualifies under domestic violence laws.

Most states require the perpetrator and victim to be current or former spouses, living together, or have a child in common.

A significant number of states include current or former dating relationships in domestic violence laws.

Delaware, Montana and South Carolina specifically exclude same-sex relationships in their domestic violence laws.

To find more information on the domestic violence laws in your state, visit www.womenslaw.org.
STATE DOMESTIC VIOLENCE LAWS
IF YOU NEED HELP

For more information or to get help, please call:
THE NATIONAL IDOMESTIC IVIOLENCE IHOTLINE Iat *1-800-799-7233*
THE NATIONAL SEXUAL ASSAULT HOTLINE AT *1-800-656-4673*
THE NATIONAL TEEN DATING ABUSE HOTLINE AT *1-866-331-9474*
PROTECTION ORDERS
REPORTING RATES
Domestic violence is one of the most chronically underreported crimes.20

Only approximately one-quarter of all physical assaults, one-fifth of all rapes, and one-half of all stalkings perpetuated against females by intimate partners are reported to the police.1

Approximately 20% of the 1.5 million people who experience intimate partner violence annually obtain civil protection orders.1

Approximately one-half of the orders obtained by women against intimate partners who physically assaulted them were violated.1 More than two-thirds of the restraining orders against intimate partners who raped or stalked the victim were violated.

The Public Policy Office of the National Coalition Against Domestic Violence (NCADV) is a national leader in the effort to create and influence Federal legislation that positively affects the lives of domestic violence victims and children. We work closely with advocates at the local, state and national level to identify the issues facing domestic violence victims, their children and the people who serve them and to develop a legislative agenda to address these issues. NCADV welcomes you to join us in our effort to end domestic violence.

www.ingramcontent.com/pod-product-compliance
Lightning Source LLC
Chambersburg PA
CBHW072205090426
42740CB00012B/2392